IRELAND

ITS MYTHS ———— AND LEGENDS

MetroBooks

Ray Gietzelt

IRELAND
ITS MYTHS ———— AND LEGENDS

MetroBooks

An Imprint of Friedman/Fairfax Publishers

Library of Congress Cataloging-in-Publication Data

Retzlaff, Kay.
    Ireland : its myths and legends / by Kay Retzlaff.
        p.   cm.
    Includes bibliographical references and index.
    ISBN 1-56799-564-0
    1. Mythology, Celtic.   2. Legends—Ireland.   I. Title.
    BL980.I7R47   1998
398.2'09415—DC21

                                                    97-36156

Editors: Tony Burgess and Ann Kirby
Designer: Milagros Sensat
Photography Editor: Karen Barr
Production Manager: Jeanne Hutter

Color separations by Fine Arts Repro House Co., Ltd
Printed in England by Butler & Tanner Limited
10 9 8 7 6 5 4 3 2 1
For bulk purchases and special sales, please contact:
Friedman /Fairfax Publishers
Attention: Sales Department
15 West 26th Street
New York, NY 10010
212/685-6610   FAX 212/685-1307

Visit our website:
http://www.metrobooks.com

To Angelica, mo chara.

Contents

Introduction

Inside the central post office in downtown Dublin, where bullet holes from the 1916 Easter Uprising that led to Irish independence still mark the walls, a Bronze Age warrior stands in silence, chained to a rock. Sword in hand, he is ready for battle even though wounds have claimed his life. His name is CúChulainn (pronounced koo-HULL-in), and he transcends the ages. CúChulainn was forged as a testament to those who gave their lives in the 1916 uprising, a reminder to twentieth-century Ireland of its mythic past. Although Dubliners pass the statue daily, usually paying little heed, this warrior's story is part of a cycle of mythological stories that have shaped the Irish spirit and nation for fifteen hundred years.

Stories of Irish mythology fueled the poetic fires of the twentieth century's great Irish poet William Butler Yeats. They sparked a resurgent interest in the Irish language. And they lit the imagination of Patrick Pearse, a leader of the Easter Uprising.

Some of the greatest tragedies in Western literature trace their roots to Irish mythology—from King Arthur and the Knights of the Round Table to King Lear. The great Irish stories are about warriors and lovers, betrayal and duty, rights and responsibilities. They are filled with boasting, bawdiness, and of course tragedy. Irish lovers are usually star-crossed, rivaling Shakespeare's Romeo and Juliet. Irish mythology also gives us some of the most notable female characters of the ancient world. These Irish Amazons are bold, dauntless, and brave—in love and war.

Scholars divide the Irish stories into four cycles: Mythological, Ulster, Fenian, and Kingly. The Mythological Cycle looks at the stories of the waves of invaders from prehistoric time. The Ulster Cycle deals primarily with stories of the Ulster hero CúChulainn, as well as such mythic tales as "The Táin Bó Cuailnge" (toyne boh COOL-ney), which means "The Cattle Raid of Cooley." The Ulster Cycle also tells of King Conchobor (KON-hov-ur) and the Red Branch champions. The Fenian Cycle focuses on Finn mac Cumhail (finn mac comoll),

Oisín (OH-sheen), and the fiana (FEE-nuh). The Kingly Cycle traces the roots of the ruling houses, primarily the house of Ui Neill (O'Neill).

The stories weren't written down until the introduction of the Western alphabet and writing in the fifth century, following the arrival of Christianity in Ireland. Before that, ogham (AUK-am), a method of making slash marks on the edges of standing stones, was used to record short inscriptions. These stories are greatly influenced by Celtic culture. (Celts is pronounced kelts; there is no soft /c/ in the Irish language. So, although the basketball team is the Boston /S/eltics, the people whose culture stretches from modern Turkey to Ireland were /K/elts.) The Celts were relative latecomers to Ireland, not arriving until around 300 B.C.E. (Before the Common Era). Their stories were written down by Irish Christian monks who may have retained an allegiance to pre-Christian ways.

What we know about Irish mythology comes from stories contained in manuscripts dating from the twelfth century. But the language of the written myths reflects a much older reality. Some scholars ascribe the details of "The Táin Bó Cuailnge," for example, to the eighth century or earlier. The stories, like those of Greece's Homer, have the flavor of tales that were told orally.

The stories are written in Old Irish, a branch of Gaelic, which is a member of the Indo-European language family. Old Irish is one of the so-called Q-Celtic languages. Scots and Manx are the other two. Thus, mac (son) and equos (horse) have the q sound. In the P-Celtic languages—Welsh, Cornish, and Breton—son is mapp and horse is epos. Old Irish entered Ireland around 300 B.C.E. It spread from there to Scotland and the Isle of Man. Irish was spoken well into the seventeenth century, but started to die out when the English crushed the Irish aristocracy. It became the language of the poor, who either died or emigrated during the potato famine of the mid-nineteenth century. Old Irish is still spoken in the Gaeltacht areas of western Ireland, but television, tourism, and economics are taking their toll.

Much of the oral mythological material must have been lost. There are no stories of the creation of the world or human beings, for example. We know very little about the gods and goddesses of Irish Celtic mythology. What we do know about them comes from the handful of Irish and Welsh stories that still exist, from archaeological evidence, from a few statues with names written on them, and from descriptions made by outsiders who weren't exactly friendly to the Irish or their culture. (Julius Caesar wrote about the Celts, but tried to fit their mythology into the Roman cosmology and religious system, without much success. He also described them harshly in a book he wrote after a campaign of what today would be called genocide against the Celts of western Europe.) The Christian writer Gerald of Wales also described Irish religious and ritual life. Both men saw the Irish as barbarians.

In the early Irish world, words were powerful. They could create and destroy. Kings were afraid of satirists, for example, because they could blight cattle and crops with their words. The druids, who were the religious leaders of the Irish Celts, and the fili, the professional poets and storytellers of Celtic Ireland, were as powerful as kings. If the stories were written down, their words would be trapped and available to all, which would weaken their power.

Caesar never conquered Ireland, but Ireland was far from being insulated against outside influences. After the ice sheets of the Paleolithic era (100,000 to 15,000 years ago) had receded, Ireland and Britain were still connected. Prehistoric hunters in Britain left behind flint tools. There were no permanent human inhabitants, but there were hunting camps as humans followed herds of giant deer. Around six thousand years before the time of Christ, water levels rose, cutting off Ireland from the rest of Europe. But people from Denmark crossed into Britain over a land bridge, then forded the straits separating the newly made island from Britain. These people settled in the district of lakes and fertile land of present-day Ulster. They lived in round huts with central hearths, which some of the Irish myths describe.

The development of farming in the Near East around 5000 B.C.E. created a demand for land. People migrated, spreading out

PREVIOUS PAGE: The love triangle of King Arthur, Guinevere, and Lancelot is reminiscent of the Irish story of Gráinne and Diarmuid. ABOVE: The slashes on the ogham stone, Coláiste Íde, Co. Kerry, are based on the Latin alphabet.

from the Mediterranean into Spain, France, Great Britain, the Netherlands, and Ireland by 3000 B.C.E. These new immigrants to Ireland built houses with wooden posts, turf walls, stone foundations, and thatch roofs. They used stone axes and knew the arts of spinning and weaving wool. (Spinning whorls have been found in archaeological digs.) They raised sheep. They knew how to make pottery. They grew grain, and they ate a lot of meat, including pork, mutton, and some beef. Their products were traded over great distances. For example, axes made from stone found in northern Ireland have been discovered at Lough Gur in County Limerick and in southern England.

These pre-Celtic people also knew how to build on a grand scale. Their sacrificial sites still stand in Ireland. Perhaps the most famous is Newgrange in the Valley of the Boyne River. It dates from about 3000 B.C.E. This megalithic chamber tomb was built several generations before the great pyramids of Egypt. We can gather a few details about the religious life of these people from the archaeological evidence gathered at the site.

Newgrange faces the rising sun. On the shortest day of the year, the sun shines through an opening above the lintel and lights up an internal chamber all the way to the central altar (there are three altars).

The stones arranged in front of the door are carved with spiral patterns that in the Mediterranean region are representative of the great goddess. (These spirals are often seen as symbolic snakes—striking evidence, given that snakes never made it to Ireland, the story of Saint Patrick notwithstanding. Perhaps the snakes Saint Patrick is said to have driven from Ireland were the remnants of an ancient goddess religion.) A great number of animal bones have been found outside the tomb, primarily those of oxen. There are also sheep, pig, horse, and dog bones in the debris. Human bones were also found inside the structure, leading researchers to believe that the site was used for sacrifices.

Following the megalithic builders were gold diggers and metal workers. As early as 2000 B.C.E., prospectors were mining and creating a gold trade with the Continent. Trade items, such as faience beads, have been traced to origins in Egypt and the Near East.

The Celtic Irish who arrived seventeen hundred years later accepted the land they found as sacred landscape. In the myths of the Celtic Irish, Newgrange is called Brug na Bóinne (brew nuh BOY-nya). It is the home of the goddess Boann (the Boyne River). It is a magical, mysterious, and terrifying place in Irish myth. Great mythological battles took place here on Samhain (SAH-win), the great religious holiday of the Celtic New Year. Newgrange was still a sacred site at the time of Roman Britain, as evidenced by the Roman coins found in the sacrificial pits. Smaller graves are spread over the Irish landscape, each of the dolmens marking them is made of three enormous slabs of stone with a capstone.

The Celts themselves originated in the Steppes. They domesticated the horse, the first weapon of mass destruction, and proceeded to spread from present-day Turkey throughout Europe to Ireland. Celts spread across Europe in migratory waves. Celtic tribes sacked Rome in 390 B.C.E. and Delphi in 279 B.C.E. They were cattle herders, constantly on the prowl for better pastures. The Celtic push into Ireland was followed by waves of other invaders—Vikings, Norman French, and the English. Each group left an imprint on the Irish psyche and mythology.

The Irish heroic stories may remind readers of Homer's *Iliad*, but it would be a mistake to assume that the world described in Irish myth is similar to that of the ancient Greeks. Unlike the deities of Greek mythology, Irish gods and goddesses are born, they live, and they die. That, however, does not mean they aren't eternal, for in Irish myth it is the Great Cycle which is eternal: birth, growth, and death. Death is not seen as an end, but as a transition. Nature, for example, does not cease to exist in the fall—fall is simply a period of gestation.

The ancient Irish saw nature as being animated by spirit, and spirit is eternal. It is only the forms that vary.

BELOW: Poet W.B. Yeats saw Ireland as Cathleen ní Houlihan, an old woman made young through the willing sacrifice of young men. (In his later years, he wrote in this tower.

Thus, there are many stories of shape shifters in Irish myth: that which is today a human, may tomorrow be a salmon or a swan. Because of the spiritual ties binding together all of nature, each warrior had to be very careful that he not alienate the spirits of nature. Many of those spirits animated animals, and therefore a great number of rules applied to human interaction with animals. For example, because his name meant hound, CúChulainn could not eat dog. Similarly, Conaire was forbidden to hunt animals, and Diarmuid was forbidden to hunt boar. And because fate could not be cheated, invariably each hero was forced to break his geis (taboo), which doomed him.

The social and political structure of ancient Ireland also differed greatly from the ancient societies of Greece and Rome. Although the land was ruled by kings, in early times that position was an elected one, as evidenced by the gathering's voting on whether Fergus could regain the kingship which he had sold in order to marry Nes, Conchobor's mother.

There were, in fact, three types of kingship—that over a single tuath, that over several tuatha, and that over a province. A tuath was a petty kingdom; the Irish word simply means "people." Each tuath was composed of various fine, or clans. The fine consisted of five generations of a family, traced through the male line. The entire clan was responsible for the misdeeds of each of its members, and for collecting blood debts if a member of the fine was killed.

By the seventh and eighth centuries of the common era, there were nearly 150 tuatha in Ireland, yet the population of the island was less than half a million people. There was no centralized government, not even the city-states found in the Greek stories. In fact, there were no

BELOW: Shakespeare's KING LEAR may have been loosely based on the Irish tale, The Fate of the Children of Lir. OPPOSITE: The Hill of Tara, Co. Meath, had been the sacred seat of kings since 2000 B.C.E.

cities in Ireland until the coming of the Vikings (although Ptolemy of Alexandria did record Emain Macha as a city on his second-century B.C.E. map). Because there was no centralized government, it became imperative to create bonds that would tie members of the tuath together. Fosterage, thus, became a vital component to societal stability. So, as we see in the story of CúChulainn's birth and fosterage, it is the king's sister who takes over the raising of the boy. In a society where the lineage was traced through the male line, fosterage of brothers' children by the sister's family created an emotional, if not a blood, tie. These relationships were governed by rules similar to those relating to the fine. In one story, not included in this collection, CúChulainn slays his foster brother in battle. This deed, a horrible breaking of a taboo, doomed the hero.

The kingships of ancient Ireland were quite different from common notions of royalty. Position was not determined by birthright and was not guaranteed. The king had to be both physically and morally perfect. Thus, Nuada, in the Mythological Cycle, loses his kingship after his hand is cut off in battle. Bres, on the other hand, is driven from the kingship of the Tuatha Dé Danaan on moral grounds, having taxed his subjects into poverty and broken all the rules of etiquette. The job of the king was to lead his people in war and to preside over a regular assembly of his tuath. Such assemblies would take care of public and private business, and also involved games and horse racing, survivals of ancient funeral games. The gathering sites were generally ancient tribal cemeteries. The king was not a judge, nor could he

enact laws: those jobs were overseen by the brehons (lawyers). And, as in the story of the birth of Conchobor, the assembly could choose a new king, just as the people chose Conchobor to replace Fergus.

The king united with the Goddess in order to ensure the fertility of the land and its creatures. Kings were both born and made. A man's heritage was as important as his deeds, and vice versa. However, without "marriage" to the Goddess, a man could not rule. So, for example, Art could not assume the kingship upon the death of his father, Cormac, until he had mated with Medb. Only through sexual union (a consummated marriage) between the king and the Goddess would the land blossom. The Goddess in Ireland had many names—Anu or Danu, Medb, Banba, the Hag of Beara, Bridget, Cathleen ní Houlihan—but her three main roles seldom varied. She gave life, she nurtured life, and she took life. The life giver was often represented as the beautiful young maiden, while the nurturer was shown to be a fecund matron, like Macha in The Twins of Macha. The taker of life aspect of the goddess was depicted as the old woman who required the blood of young warriors to return to her youthful self.

These stories are the heritage of the Irish. They were considered so precious that they were written down, even though the society these stories represented shunned writing for fear that the power of the words would be stolen. In order to preserve them, the stories were told to Christian scribes, who put the names and stories down in ink. Later scribes transferred, compiled, edited, amended, and added to those stories. The stories live as long as they are told.

PART 1

THE MYTHOLOGICAL CYCLE

ccording to the *Book of Invasions*, the first people in Ireland were the Partholonians. They were followed by the Nemedians; the Fir Bolg (fear borg), who were the men of the bellows (miners with smelters, perhaps); and the Tuatha Dé Danann (TOO-ah-tha Jé DON-un), the people of the goddess Danu, or Anu. According to the stories, the Tuatha Dé came from northern Europe, where they learned the druidic arts. The Sons of Mil, who are reputed to have come from Spain, followed the Tuatha Dé into Ireland, literally driving them underground into the world of the Sídh (shee).

The Sídh is badly translated as "fairy mound." Fairies, or the wee people, are seen today as tricksters, though not necessarily harmful. There is a great deal more to the Sídh folk than that. For one thing, they are the same size as humans. Their society is organized very much like that of the cattle-herding Celtic people of Ireland. They are very powerful. One way of looking at the Sídh folk is to consider them as beings living in a parallel universe. The worlds of the Sídh and of humans can collide at any point when one thing becomes another, such as dawn into day, dusk into night, and spring into summer, but especially at Samháin, the Celtic New Year. Others in the West celebrate this most sacred of holidays as All Hallowe's Eve, or Halloween.

Coexisting with the Tuatha Dé was a group called the Fomorians, who lived under the ocean waves. These people were the alter egos of the Tuatha Dé. The Fomorians and the Tuatha Dé formed alliances through intermarriage. They vied for sovereignty over Ireland until the Second Battle of Mag Tuired, wherein the Tuatha Dé decisively defeated the Fomorians.

Just as the world was divided into different realms, so, too, was time. The Irish Celtic year is divided into fourths: Samháin is November 1; Imbolc (IM-bolorg) is February 1; Beltane (BEL-tun-uh) is May 1; and Lughnasa (LOO-na-suh) is August 1. The equinoxes and solstices divide these quarters in half. The Irish Celtic quarter years are tied to the agricultural/pastoral year: spring for plowing and sowing, summer for the growth of grain, autumn for the ripening of the grain, and winter for the eating of the grain. According to myth, these holy days were created by King Bres upon his defeat by the Tuatha Dé in the Second Battle of Mag Tuired. He created the four times of year so that the victors would spare his life. These holidays were so sacred that they were taken into the Christian church year: Samháin became All Hallowe's Eve/All Saints' Day; Imbolc, the festival of Saint Brigid; Beltane, May Day; and Lughnasa, Lammas Day.

Time thus became sacred through its division and naming. Naming also created the sacred spaces of Ireland. Before their defeat by the Tuatha Dé, the Fir Bolg divided Ireland into provinces: Ulster, Leinster, Munster, and Connacht. A fifth province that existed in a separate plane was Mide—the middle, or "belly button," of Ireland. Each province also had sacred sites, which figure prominently in the myths: Ulster held Emain Macha (EV-in MA-kuh) and Brug na Bóine; Leinster, the Hill of Tara; Munster, the Paps of Anu; and Connacht, Cruachán and Mag Tuired.

The Second Battle of Mag Tuired

Smoke and mist from burning ships so filled the air the day the Tuatha Dé Danaan landed on the west coast of Ireland in Connemara, that the people living in Ireland thought the invaders came in clouds. In fact, the people of the goddess Danu had burned their ships to keep anyone of their company who was faint of heart from running away from the impending battle. For, you see, the Tuatha Dé intended to conquer and claim Ireland for themselves.

In the first battle of Mag Tuired, the Tuatha Dé defeated the Fir Bolg, the inhabitants of Ireland. The Tuatha Dé killed many, including the king of the Men of the Bellows, and took over the sovereignty of Ireland.

But during the battle, Nuada, the king of the Tuatha Dé, had his hand chopped off. According to Tuatha Dé law, the king must be unblemished. The great physician Dian Cécht fitted Nuada with a silver hand that worked as well as a real hand, but the women of the Tuatha Dé protested.

"He is blemished," they said. "The king must be perfect. Nuada has lost his hand. He must give up the kingship."

The men of the Tuatha Dé had to give in.

"Let us choose Bres the Beautiful to be the king of the Tuatha Dé," said the women. "He is our foster son. His mother, Ériu, is one of us."

The assembly agreed and chose Bres the Beautiful to be king in place of the disfigured Nuada. This proved to be the beginning of an evil time. Bres' loyalty to the Tuatha Dé was questionable. His father was a Fomorian, one of the kings of the people who lived beneath the waves. When Bres assumed the kingship, the Fomorians laid claim to the land of the Tuatha Dé—at least that is what Bres told the Tuatha Dé. The Tuatha Dé were kept in poverty and the champions of the Tuatha Dé were forced into labor to pay the tribute that Bres demanded.

Ogma, the god of poetry, had to carry firewood. The Dagda, the god of plenty, built the walls and trenches of Bres' fortress. To add insult to injury, King Bres' blind satirist, Cridenbel, claimed the three choicest parts of the Dagda's dinner every night. In those days the satirist had great power, as much power as a king. A satirist's words could wither crops and herds. King Bres' satirist was an ugly man. His mouth was in his chest and his appetite seemed unquenchable. The three bits he took from the Dagda each night were each the size of a pig. As a result, the poor Dagda was wasting away.

One day, as the Dagda was digging trenches outside the walls of Bres' fortress, the Dagda's son, the young god Oengus Mac Óc, stopped to talk.

"The work is looking good," said the Mac Óc. "But what makes you look so bad?"

The Dagda moaned and told his tale of trouble to his son. He told how Cridenbel, the man with the unappeasable appetite, laid claim to the greater portion of each night's dinner.

The Mac Óc thought the problem over. "I have an idea that will rid you of Cridenbel and may free us from the Fomorians at the same time. Take these," he said, handing his father three pieces of gold. "Mix them into your three choicest tidbits at dinner tonight.

When Cridenbel lays claim to the tidbits, give them to him. He will eat the gold with the food, and this will kill him. When Cridenbel dies, people will say that you have poisoned him and King Bres will order you killed. This will be his undoing, for in so doing he will have made a false judgement." In those days a king could be deposed for making a bad judgement.

The young god continued, "When King Bres orders you killed, you must protest and prove that you did nothing wrong. Custom demands that you give to the satirist what he demands. Explain that you hid the three gold coins in your food because you had no other place. Then, when Cridenbel demanded those three pieces of food, you were required by our custom to give them to him. Thus, the satirist killed himself through his greed. King Bres will order the satirist cut open and the gold retrieved to see if you tell the truth."

It happened exactly as the Mac Óc had foreseen. Soon thereafter ill will festered among the chiefs of the Tuatha Dé, and they started complaining aloud of King Bres' treatment when they sat together.

"I have yet to taste the succulent flavor of roast pork at King Bres' table, nor have I sipped a soothing draft of ale," said the Dagda.

"A man could starve during a visit to the king, if he doesn't die of thirst first."

The company laughed and nodded their heads in agreement.

"It's a toss-up, then," said Ogma. "I fear boredom may kill a man before starvation or thirst. King Bres is a stingy man, an evil thing in a king. I have yet to be paid for entertaining guests of the king. He does not hire poets, bards, satirists, harpers, pipers, jugglers, or fools to entertain his guests, as the rules of etiquette demand."

They all nodded glumly.

"He doesn't even provide athletic contests," said Credne, the brazier, incredulously. "I ask you, how are warriors to stay in shape without athletic contests? This is an evil thing that leads to weakness."

"You complain of trifles," sniffed Cairbre, the chief satirist. "As you know, a satirist is the equal of any king. My words can create the world or destroy it." Cairbre looked around the circle and all nodded agreement.

"That is so," said the Dagda.

"I was treated in the most insulting manner when I paid the visit required of me by custom," Cairbre said. "Is it not so that I should have eaten with the king and slept on a bed equal to his, as is the tradition regarding the treatment of the satirist?"

"This is so," said Ogma.

"Well, I received no such welcome. You should have seen with what insolence I was treated," Cairbre said. "My room' was a narrow little cabin in which there was no light or furniture or even a bed, for that matter."

"This is not possible," said the Dagda.

"I tell you, I do not lie," said Cairbre. "But wait, the tale gets worse. For food I received only three small, dry cakes!"

ABOVE: Prehistoric Dún Aengus, the Fort of Oengus, sits on Inishmore, the biggest of the Aran Islands, in Galway Bay.

OPPOSITE: Picturesque Kilmacduagh Abbey, a girl's school today, nestles in the hills of Connemara, the land of Ailill and Medb.

"What did you do?" asked Credne curiously.

"I did what I had to do to rid us of this avaricious king," said Cairbre. "I did what custom demanded, for, as you know, a king without largesse curses his people to poverty and ruin.

"After spending a sleepless night in that dank, dark hovel with no bed, I rose at dawn and cursed King Bres. He will not trouble us much longer," said Cairbre.

His companions looked at one another and smiled, lifted their glasses, and toasted each other. "Slainte," said all. "Health!"

From that time on, King Bres lost all that he had—all because of his niggardly treatment of Cairbre. Cows ceased giving milk. Crops rotted in the fields. As a result, the Tuatha Dé voted to take from Bres the right of kingship. Bres begged to serve out seven years. The assembly of the Tuatha Dé agreed, but demanded that Bres collect no taxes or rents during that time. King Bres reluctantly agreed. He went to his mother, Eriu, and pleaded for help.

"Mother, the Tuatha Dé have stripped me of the kingship," Bres complained. "Who am I to turn to?"

"Perhaps your father can aid you," said Eriu. "We will ask."

Eriu took Bres over the waves to meet his father, Elatha, a king of the Fomorians.

"What has brought you out of the land of Ireland?" asked Elatha of his son.

Bres boasted to his father, "I have become very rich. I took every-thing from my subjects, even their food. I am a powerful man, but the Tuatha Dé have stripped me of my title of king. I must give it up at the end of seven years."

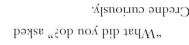
ABOVE: Sun glints through a stone wall in Burren, Co. Clare.
OPPOSITE: The castles of Ireland, like that of Kildemy, are a legacy left by the Normans.

Elatha shook his head in disappointment. "This is bad," he told his son. "A king's duty is to see to the prosperity of his people. A good king seeks the prayers of his people, not their curses. Why have you come here?"

"I need your help, Father."

Bres replied, "If you provide troops, I can regain my kingship, taking it by force from the Tuatha Dé."

"You shouldn't take by force what you lost through injustice," said Elatha.

"If you won't help me," said Bres, "I will find others who will."

Bres went to other kings of the Fomorians and appealed to their avarice. He promised to give the wealth of Ireland to them if they helped him retain the kingship. Bres spent the seven years the Tuatha Dé had given him raising an army in order to try to keep the kingship by force.

The Tuatha Dé did not remain idle, however, for they knew what Bres was up to. They chose Lug of the Long Arm as the next king because of the many talents he possessed. Lug spent the seven years organizing his troops.

He asked each of the gods what they would bring to the upcoming battle.

Each rose before the assembly and swore an oath.

Goibniu, the smith, promised that for every spear or weapon that needed repair, he would provide a new weapon. He also swore that every spear point that he cast in his forge would fly true and kill the enemy.

Dian Cécht, the great physician, promised that every man in their army who was wounded, unless his head were cut off or the brain membrane or spinal marrow severed, would be cured and ready to fight the very next day. He, his two sons, Octriul and Miach, and his daughter, Airmed, sang spells over the well of Slane so that mortally wounded men who were cast into it as soon as they were slain would be healed and come out alive.

Credne, the brazier, promised that he would provide rivets for spears and sword hilts, and bosses and rims for the shields.

Luchta, the wright, promised to provide all the shields and javelin hafts that the Tuatha Dé host required.

Ogma, the champion of the Tuatha Dé, promised to repel Bres and to capture a third of his men.

Mathgen, the sorcerer, promised to cast the mountains of Ireland onto the Fomorians. He promised, too, that the twelve great mountains of Ireland would support the Tuatha Dé in the coming battle.

The chief cupbearer of the Tuatha Dé promised that he would bring the twelve great lakes and the twelve great rivers of Ireland together so that the Fomorians would find not a drink of water in all of Ireland.

Figol, the druid, promised to rain showers of fire down upon the Fomorian host, thus taking away two-

BELOW: The Dingle Peninsula, Co. Kerry, is a place of green, rolling hills. The twin hills, the Paps of (the goddess) Anu, are in Kerry. OPPOSITE: According to tradition, Dun Aengus was built by the Fir Bolg, vanquished by the Tuatha Dé Danaan.

thirds of the Fomorians' valor, bravery, and strength. He promised, too, to bind their urine in their bodies and those of their horses. The Tuatha Dé, on the other hand, would breathe in bravery and valor with every breath that they took.

Cairbre, the satirist, promised a satire on the Fomorians that would so shame them that they would not be able to resist the warriors of the Tuatha Dé.

Be-culle and Dianann, the two witches, promised to enchant the trees, stones, and sod of Ireland so that the very land would rout the enemy, filling them with horror and trembling.

The Dagda promised that the great power of his club would pound the bones of the Fomorians into dust.

The Morrígu, the three battle goddesses, promised to give the Tuatha Dé vigor on the field of battle.

After seven years had passed, the day came when Bres, leading the Fomorian host, invaded Ireland. The Fomorians marched out to meet the Tuatha Dé on the plain of battle. Both sides uttered a great shout as they ran

forward into battle. There was great slaughter, but the heroes of the Tuatha Dé who fell in battle were healed in the magic waters of the Slane by Dian Cécht and his three children. The newly revived warriors returned to fight the very next day.

Goibniu kept his word, and no matter how many spears and swords were destroyed in the battle, there were new ones in their place the next day. Those among the Fomorians who fell in battle were not resurrected, and their arms were not replaced. The field became slippery with blood.

Lug of the Long Arm fought his own grandfather, Balor, a king of the Fomorians. Balor was known for his evil eye, which could destroy all that it looked on. Lug cast a sling-stone through his grandfather's evil eye, thus killing him.

The Morrigu, as promised, flew over the field of battle, urging the Tuatha Dé to their best efforts. The Tuatha Dé won the battle, taking Bres captive.

"Mercy," Bres begged. "Spare my life and I will give you a boon. I will renounce all claims to Ireland, and I and the Fomorians will leave it forever."

"This is not enough," said Lug. "You have lost the battle. You give us nothing that we haven't won."

"I swear all the cows of Ireland will give milk," said Bres.

"This is not enough to spare you," said Lug. "What else can you offer?"

"I will divide the year into fourths so that there will be a harvest of grain in every quarter. Thus, there will be spring for plowing and sowing, summer for strengthening the grain, fall for the ripening and reaping of the grain, and winter for consuming the grain."

"This is good," said Lug.

The gods accepted Bres' ransom and so the year was created.

The Morrigu flew over the battle, singing a song of victory and placing a blessing of peace on the Tuatha Dé.

The Wooing of Étaín

In the days of the Tuatha Dé Danaan, Eochaid Airem (y-OCH-i ARE-um) took over the high kingship of Ireland. But he was lonely, for he had no wife. The year after he took the high kingship, Eochaid Airem called the people of Ireland to the Feast of Tara, which was to be held the fourteen days before Samhain and the fourteen days after. It was at the Feast of Tara that the high king collected the taxes and levies from the men of Ireland for the coming five years. But the men of Ireland refused to attend.

"We will not come to Tara," they said, "for although it is required by custom that we bring our wives to the Feast of Tara, we cannot bring our wives if the king is not married."

Eochaid Airem decided to send messengers throughout Ireland to look for a woman who could match him in beauty, grace, and lineage and who could become his wife. One day, one of his messengers came across such a woman, Étaín (AY-dean), the daughter of the king of the Sídh at Echrad. The messenger returned quickly to Eochaid Airem to tell him of his discovery.

Eochaid Airem went in search of Étaín. He found her coming from the river, where she had gone to wash her golden hair.

Eochaid thought he had never seen a lovelier sight. She wore a green silk tunic embroidered in gold, which set off her fair skin. Her teeth were straight and white, her blue eyes reflected the autumn sky. Her cheeks were rosy, her lips enticing.

"Maiden," said Eochaid Airem, "where are you from? What is your name?"

BELOW: Dunluce Castle sits in Co. Antrim, part of northern Ireland, traditionally part of Ulster. OPPOSITE: Rivers, like the Cahir, Co. Tipperary, demarcated boundaries. Fords were defended by heroes, such as CúChulainn, in single combat.

"I am Étaín, the daughter of the king of the Sídh," said she.

"Étaín," said Eochaid Airem, "I am Eochaid Airem, the high king of Ireland. I have come seeking a wife. Will you consent to marry me?"

"That is why I have come to you," said Étaín. "I have waited the twenty years since I was born in the Sídh for you to come, denying the young men of the Sídh the pleasure of my company. But you must give me my proper bride price."

"That is proper and good," said Eochaid Airem. "And you shall dwell at my fort for as long as you have desire for me. And I pledge to leave all other women and to live with you alone as long as you wish. What is your bride price?"

"Seven bond women," said Étaín. This was a high price for a bride.

"It shall be so," said Eochaid Airem.

And Étaín went with the high king to his fort, and she was made welcome by all.

With their high king married, the people of Ireland agreed to come to the Feast of Tara. Ailill (ALL-ill), the high king's brother, also came to the feast. He was himself a king of a province of Ireland. When he saw Étaín in the banquet hall, he could not keep his eyes from her face. She was the most beautiful woman he had ever seen. Ailill's wife noticed his inattention. She saw where his eyes lingered.

"Ailill, where are your thoughts?" said his wife. "You should be paying attention to me, not your brother's wife. You had best be careful that your brother does not hear these sighs of yours. You know, they say that men who sigh are in love."

Ailill blushed and looked at his wife, but did not answer her. He was ashamed of himself, and he forced himself to stop looking at Étaín, but he could not overcome his desire for her. When the other people of Ireland returned to their own homes after the Feast of Tara, Ailill tarried at Eochaid's fort, because he wanted to stay close to Étaín. Ailill's wife prepared to return to her own people.

"Stay here if you will," she said, "Bring dishonor on yourself and your brother, but I will not bear this dishonor."

Ailill knew he should accompany his wife home. But even though being so close to the beautiful Étaín, with no hope of consummating his love, made him ill, the thought of ever leaving her made him feel even sicker.

In truth, Ailill's health failed because of the turmoil in his heart. He wasted away so that his brother, the high king Eochaid Airem, feared that he would die.

"What is wrong with you?" Eochaid Airem asked.

"I swear I don't know," said Ailill.

Eochaid Airem sent for the court physician. The physician examined Ailill.

"Well," he said at last.

"What is wrong with Ailill?" asked Eochaid Airem.

"It's one of two things," the physician said. "Either he suffers from the pangs of love or of jealousy."

Ailill was more ashamed than ever, but he would not confess his love for Étaín even if it meant he would die. He would not bring such dishonor on himself or his brother, the high king.

After the doctor's visit, Eochaid Airem was forced by the duties of office to make a circuit of his kingdom.

"I fear that Ailill is dying," he told Étaín. "You must, as my wife, make sure that he is comfortable and that he has all that he desires. Will you do this?"

"As you wish," said Étaín.

While Eochaid Airem was gone visiting his subjects, Étaín went every day to minister to his dying brother. She bathed Ailill and cut up his food. Ailill seemed to get better whenever she was with him, but his health failed when she was attending to other duties.

"Is there anything you desire?" she asked one morning. "If there is anything that I can do to help you get better, please tell me, and I will do it, if I am able."

Ailill blushed at this. He could not meet her gaze. He sighed with the enormity of his disgrace. These three signs told Étaín much. She looked away and thought of the instructions left her by her husband.

"If it will bring your health back to you," Étaín said, "you must meet me tomorrow morning, and I will grant you your desire. But we must meet outside my husband's house, for I would bring no dishonor on him."

"Lady," said Ailill, "I will meet you as you ask."

Étaín left Ailill to his thoughts. He could not rest. The day was long, and he tossed and turned all through the night, tortured with thoughts of Étaín and shamed at the thought of dishonoring his

LEFT: A wooden fence marks a boundary line today. Natural boundaries, such as rivers, hills, trees, lakes, or springs marked the sacred boundaries of CuChulainn's world.

brother. As dawn neared, he fell into a deep slumber, his frail body exhausted by his inner turmoil.

Outside the fortress gates, Étaín waited. A man who looked like Ailill came to her, and they lay together, but he told her that he could not make love to her.

"Forgive me, my lady," he said. "My illness has made me weak."

Later in the day, when Étaín went to attend to Ailill, she found him weeping.

"Why so sad, my lord?" she asked.

"I am ashamed of myself," said Ailill. "I agreed to meet you this morning, my lady, but I overslept and just now awoke."

"We will meet tomorrow," said Étaín, wondering who it was that had visited her that morning.

The next morning Ailill was again deep in sleep, and the stranger in Ailill's shape kept the tryst with Étaín. This time she recognized that the stranger was not Ailill, though much like him in shape and form. She sent the stranger away. Again she visited Ailill, and he confessed that he had slept through the appointed time. They agreed to meet the third day as well. Once again, Ailill was overcome with an unnatural, deep sleep. The stranger appeared in Ailill's shape as before.

"Who are you, stranger?" Étaín demanded. "Why have you taken the form of Ailill?"

"I am Midir, my lady. We knew each other in the Sídh a long time ago," said the stranger. "I have taken Ailill's form to protect your honor and his. This enchantment would have been the ruin of you both."

"I thank you, stranger, but why have you done this for me?" asked Étaín curiously.

"I was your husband in the Sídh in ages past," replied the stranger. "You have forgotten your life in the Sídh because of an enchantment placed on you by my first wife. I am the one who put desire for you into Ailill's heart, but I have regretted this. It was done in anger, but I have no desire to injure you in this way. Will you come away with me?"

"I will not come unless my husband, the high king of Ireland, sends me away," said Étaín.

As Étaín watched, Midir pulled his cloak about him, turned into a bird, and flew up and away. From that moment, Ailill's health returned and his desire for Étaín subsided.

"This is as it should be," said Ailill. "My health has been returned, and your honor has remained intact."

Some say Midir returned not long after and took Étaín from her husband by trickery, taking her to the Sídh. They say, too, that in revenge Eochaid Airem laid siege to the Sídh of Midir, sacking the mounds. For this sacrilege, it is said, the Sídh folk haunted Eochaid Airem and his descendants.

RIGHT: *Ardbear Bay lies in Connemara. Connemara is the westernmost part of the ancient province of Connacht, the kingdom of Ailill and Medb.*

The Destruction of Da Derga's Hostel

One day the high king of Ireland, Conaire, traveled the main road of Leinster, distraught at how his country was unraveling. During the first six years of his reign, Ireland had been filled with peace and prosperity, but during the seventh year, assaults on law and order were increasing. Robbers and thieves wandered the roadways, and pirates from Scotland threatened the calm.

"My king and my foster son," said Mac Cécht, Conaire's foster father, "dusk is falling. It is time to find a bed for the night. It is unseemly that the king of Tara should roam the roads of Ireland looking for a place to eat and sleep. The nobles of Ireland should be vying to serve you. These are bad times indeed, filled with ill-mannered louts."

"I have a friend nearby," said Conaire. "He will serve us this evening."

"Who is this, my king?" asked Mac Cécht.

"Da Derga, the red-haired one," said Conaire. "He owes me much. I gave him many gifts. He will receive us with hospitality tonight."

"I know this man, my king," said Mac Cécht. "You are right. This very road will take us directly into his hostel, which is famous. Weary travelers are always met with good food, a roaring fire, and a clean bed. I have heard that the seven roads of Leinster run right into the hostel. They say it has seven doorways, with seven rooms between each doorway, and that only the door through which the wind comes is covered."

"This is so," said Conaire. "Da Derga will receive us."

"I will ride ahead to let our host know you are coming and to light a fire so that your room is warm when you arrive," said Mac Cécht.

So Mac Cécht rode ahead, leaving Conaire with his retinue and his heavy thoughts.

BELOW: A Celtic-style statue from Bohemia shows a man wearing the traditional torque and sporting a mustache. OPPOSITE: Conaire's father was a bird man of the Sídh who seduced Étaín, the third woman to bear that name.

"Why so silent, Father?" asked Le Fri Flaith, Conaire's son.

"This is an ill-fated night, my son," Conaire said.

"What fate, Father?" asked Le Fri Flaith.

"That is a long story, my son," Conaire said. "It has to do with events that happened long ago, when my great-grandfather, Eochaid Airem, destroyed the mounds of the Sídh folk in his search for my great-grandmother, Étaín, who had returned to the Sídh. Some say that the Sídh folk have an animosity against all his descendants. But there is another reason for my feelings of ill ease.

"My mother, your grandmother, was the third to carry the name of Étaín. She was married to King Eterscel, but the king was not my father. This I did not discover until it was too late."

As they rode, Conaire told his son his story.

"The first Étaín from the Sídh bore a daughter by Eochaid Airem, but no sons, before she returned to the Sídh with Midir. The daughter she left behind was named Étaín, after her mother. The second Étaín was married to Cormac, the king of Ulster. Like her mother, she bore only a daughter and no sons. This child, my mother, was also named Étaín, so there were three generations of Étaíns.

"But Cormac was unhappy being the father of a daughter. He commanded that the baby girl be killed. He ordered two servants to throw the child in a pit, but the baby smiled at the servants and they couldn't kill her. Instead they hid her in a calf shed where the cowherds of the king of Tara found her.

"My mother was raised by the cowherds, who built for her a special house of wickerwork that had no door, only a smoke hole, for they feared for her safety, and their own, should Cormac the king discover she still lived.

"One day my mother, a young maiden, looked up to see a great white speckled bird at the smoke hole of her special house. The bird flew down to her and stood on the floor. Suddenly he shed his bird skin and stood before her, a beautiful man of the Sídh.

"'Tomorrow, the king of Tara, Eterscel, will come to take you away to be his wife,' the bird man told my mother. 'Tonight I will lay with you and you shall conceive a son. You will name him Conaire, and he will be king of Tara. He will have this taboo upon him: he must not hunt birds.'

"The bird man lay with my mother. In the morning, he put on his bird skin and flew away. Later that day, King Eterscel came to my mother's special house. He was curious as to what it contained, so he sent a servant up on the roof to peer down the smoke hole.

"'My king, there is the most beautiful maiden in the world inside,' the servant said.

"Now Eterscel was without a wife, for it had been prophesied that he would marry a woman of unknown race who would give him a son who would be king. He ordered his servants to destroy the house and to take the maiden captive.

"Eterscel raised me as his son," said Conaire. "But I have failed to keep the taboos placed on me by my true father, the Bird Man of the Sídh, for my mother never told me of my patrimony."

This made Le Fri Flaith curious. "How, then, Father, did you learn the truth?" he asked.

"In my ignorance I hunted a tribe of great white speckled birds," said Conaire. "I should have suspected the truth, that these were beings from the Sídh, for although I gave chase, I could never bring a bird down with my spear. I followed them to the very waves, but they shed their bird skins and stood before me as men, armed with spears and swords. One of their number came to my defense, shielding me from their attack. He said that he was the king of my father's birds.

"It is through my ignorance of the taboo against hunting birds that I have doomed myself and my followers," lamented Conaire. "My father's steward of birds told me how to become king of Ireland, but he also told me the taboos I had to follow."

"What are these taboos, Father?"

"I am not to go clockwise around the sacred grounds of Tara, nor am I to go counterclockwise around the sacred Plain of Breg," said

ABOVE: *An aerial view of Dun Aengus shows a well-defended site, protected by sheer cliffs and rocky terrain devoid of vegetation.*
OPPOSITE: *A rocky road winds through a lonely windswept valley.*

Conaire. "I must not hunt the evil beasts of Cerna."

"Oh, Father, these are evil omens indeed," said Le Fri Flaith with despair.

He, like his father, hung his head in misery because that very day, Conaire had broken all of these dreaded taboos.

The people of the Sídh had filled the land with a heavy mist, and Conaire's troops had become disoriented while chasing the brigands who were terrorizing Ireland. In their confusion, they had broken all three of these taboos.

Pirates had burned the land of the southern O'Neills that day as well. The smoke, mingling with the mist, had hidden the sacred lands of Tara and the Plain of Breg, causing Conaire and his band of men to travel clockwise around Tara, and then counterclockwise around the Plain of Breg.

They had hunted for food in the fog, and only at the end of the chase did they find that the prey they sought were Cerna's evil beasts.

"Are these the only taboos placed on you, my father?" asked Le Fri Flaith. "Perhaps there are others, more powerful, and if you keep them, these small offenses will not damn you."

"Maybe you are right, my son," said Conaire. But as he spoke, three horsemen, dressed in red and each with long red hair, approached on three roan horses and passed them. Conaire's face went white at the sight of them.

"What is it, Father?" asked Le Fri Flaith. "What is it that has frightened you?"

"I am forbidden by my taboos to let three reds precede me to the house of red," said Conaire with concern. "Da Derga has red hair, you see. If we follow those three red riders to Da Derga's hostel, I will break yet another taboo. We must stop those men."

"I will ride after them, Father, and ask that they ride behind us, so that you do not break your taboo," said Le Fri Flaith.

The young man lashed his horse and rode off after the men dressed in red, but he could not overtake them no matter how fast his horse ran. The three riders remained always the same distance ahead.

"Wait! Stop!" yelled Le Fri Flaith. "I must speak with you. You must not go before the king."

The three riders dressed in red did not stop, but one of the men yelled over his shoulder as he rode on, "There is great news from the hostel, my son."

Le Fri Flaith returned to his father and told him what the riders had said.

"This is not good," said Conaire. "Offer them three oxen, three pigs, and a seat close to the fire for as long as they tarry with us. Hurry, offer this to them."

So Le Fri Flaith sped off in chase. But, as before, he could not gain on the three horsemen dressed in red. He could get only as close as shouting distance, and no closer.

"My father offers you three oxen, three pigs, and choice seats beside the fire," Le Fri Flaith shouted, "only you must not precede the king to the hostel."

One of the men shouted over his shoulder, "Great news, my son. Ancient enchantments will burn you."

Le Fri Flaith turned back to his father and repeated the message.

"Offer them six oxen, six pigs, and gifts, as well as good seats by the fire," said Conaire. "Hurry. We are close to the hostel." Le Fri Flaith sped away toward the three riders but could not gain on them.

"My father offers you six oxen, six pigs, gifts, and good seats by the fire," yelled Le Fri Flaith. "In return, he asks only that you do not precede the king to the hostel."

The third man yelled over his shoulder, "We come from the Sídh. We may be alive, but we are sentenced to death. There will be destruction, death, blood. Beware sundown, my son."

Le Fri Flaith returned to his father.

"You could not detain them, then," said Conaire.

"It isn't because I didn't try, Father," said Le Fri Flaith. He told his father what the man had said.

"It is as I feared. I am cursed," said Conaire. "My fate is sealed. The enmity of the folk of the Sídh is not yet appeased."

As Conaire and his retinue approached Da Derga's hostel, they could see the light from the hearth fires. The three men dressed in red had descended from their horses and entered the hostel.

"I have broken all my taboos this day," sighed Conaire. They dismounted at the hostel. A beastly man approached, with an ugly hag

RIGHT: An ancient text refers to the king of Cashel as the high king of Ireland. Cashel became an important center for Christianity.

following behind him. The man was tall, but stoop-shouldered. His hair was black and stood up in great spikes. He carried a pig, its hair singed by fire, over his shoulder.

"Welcome, King Conaire," said the man. "We have been expecting you for a long time. I have brought you this swine for your dinner tonight."

"Please, tonight is not good. Perhaps we can eat together some other time."

"That will not be possible, King Conaire," said the ugly man. "It must be tonight."

A heavy-hearted Conaire and his retinue followed the man with the pig into the hostel. Da Derga, the red-haired hostler, bid them welcome and seated them by the fire. The three men dressed in red sat next to the wall and nodded at Conaire as he came in.

"Welcome, King Conaire," said Da Derga. "You are welcome here. Your reign has brought peace and prosperity. The sun has shone from the beginning of spring until the end of autumn. The dew has been heavy and the wind mild. Grain has been plentiful. The oak mast has been heavy, and the pigs fat as a result. The wolves have been kept in abeyance—until now. I fear that the wolves are at the door this night, my king."

What he said was true. The men who preyed like wolves on the kingdom had followed King Conaire to the hostel. Among them were men of Ireland who had refused to give up stealing cattle and thieving during the reign of Conaire, and who had been driven from Ireland. They had fled to Scotland and the Islands, where they had met with ruffians of evil intent. The leader of this evil band was Ingcel, a man so immoral he had murdered his own mother and father and all seven of his brothers. Ingcel had only one eye in his head and hatred in his heart, and he was greatly feared by his own men.

Ingcel and his evil band had returned to Ireland to wreak havoc on the land, and now they were but a short distance from the hostel. The flames from their fires were just visible to the beleaguered king as he sought shelter.

"What is that?" asked Conaire from his seat beside the fire. "What is that light from the darkness?"

"Warriors approaching the hostel," said Mac Cécht.

The king and his men leaped up and grabbed their weapons. Rushing out into the darkness, they captured and beheaded one of Ingcel's spies. Conaire threw the head out into the darkness; Ingcel threw it back into the hostel. Three times the spy's head was tossed back and forth. Then the battle burst into full fever.

The bloody battle raged for hours. Arms were hacked off. Heads were separated from the shoulders of warriors. Blood made the earth

LEFT: The Clifden Sky Road winds along Ardbear Bay in modern Connemara, Co. Galway. Connemara was part of Connacht, the kingdom of Ailill and Medb.

37

THE MYTHOLOGICAL CYCLE

slippery. Conaire's men tried to protect him from harm, but he forged into the thick of the fray at every opportunity.

The work of battle filled Conaire with a great thirst. He retreated to the hostel with Mac Cécht and Le Fri Flaith following behind him, protecting his retreat.

"A drink," said Conaire. "I die of thirst. I must have a drink."

"At once, my king," said Mac Cécht. He searched the hostel for water, but could find none. He found a scullery boy and demanded water for the king.

"My lord, there is none," said the boy. "We used all the water to put out the fires that the men of darkness set, trying to burn the hostel to the ground. There isn't a drop of water to be had anywhere."

Mac Cécht returned to the king and told him the boy's news.

"I must have a drink," said Conaire. "I die of thirst."

"I will find you water," Mac Cécht said.

ABOVE: Stone walls and the ruins of a house guard the hillside overlooking Ardbear Bay in Connemara, on the west coast of Ireland.
OPPOSITE: Despite punishing wind and rain, Celtic crosses remain standing in an Aran Island cemetery that is more than a thousand years old.

Mac Cécht grabbed Conaire's golden drinking cup, which was the size of a large ox. He motioned Le Fri Flaith to follow him, and they fought their way out of the hostel and broke free. They fled toward the river, searching for water, but it was dry. They searched and searched. Morning was nearly breaking, and they had found the twelve rivers of Ireland as well as the twelve main lakes bone dry. At last they found water at a spring flowing on the sacred Plain of Ai. Mac Cécht filled the king's cup, and he and Le Fri Flaith hurried back to the hostel.

Smoke filled the air above the hostel. As Mac Cécht and Le Fri Flaith crested the last hill before the hostel, they saw bodies strewn across the plain. Black crows plucked at the corpses. And before them were two men cutting off the head of Conaire.

"My king!" cried Mac Cécht.

"Father!" wailed Le Fri Flaith.

The men of darkness looked up from their grisly task. One threw a pillar stone at Mac Cécht. The other grabbed Conaire's head and ran.

Mac Cécht picked up the pillar stone and heaved it at the running man. The stone cracked the man's spine, killing him instantly. Mac Cécht ran to Conaire's head. He poured the water he carried into the king's mouth and on his neck. The head of Conaire spoke to him.

"You're a good man, Mac Cécht. An excellent man. You have given your king a drink. This was a noble deed, Mac Cécht."

Mac Cécht and Le Fri Flaith pursued the few men remaining from the evil band and killed them all. But Le Fri Flaith was slain in the heat of battle, and Mac Cécht was horribly wounded. For three days he lay on the battlefield. On the third day, a woman walked across the battlefield.

"Oh, woman," cried Mac Cécht. "Please come to me."

"I will not cross this horrible place," she said.

"No harm will come to you, I swear," said Mac Cécht.

The woman crossed the battlefield then. As she walked, crows eating the flesh of slain warriors jumped away.

"Please, help me," said Mac Cécht as she came near. "There is an ant torturing me. It bites at my wound. Please, pull it off me."

What Mac Cécht thought was an ant was really a wolf, which had buried its snout in his wound. The woman pulled the wolf off Mac Cécht, who grabbed the wolf by its throat and killed it with a single blow to its forehead. With the help of the woman, Mac Cécht cleaned his wound. He then carried the body of Conaire upon his back and Conaire's head under his arm all the way to Tara. He buried Conaire there, as befitted a king. Afterward, Mac Cécht returned to Connemara, his own country, to be cured of his wounds.

The Twins of Macha

There lived in Ulster a man named Crunniuc. He lived in the hills, hidden in the wild places, with his sons. His wife had died, and he had no one to oversee his household.

One day, while he was alone, there came to his house a beautiful woman. She walked in as though she had always been there. That night she slept with Crunniuc, and from then on, stayed with him as his wife.

The mysterious woman seemed to bring good fortune to Crunniuc and his household. After she came to live with Crunniuc, there was always food in the larder and on the table. The clothes she made were finely woven and sewn. Everything in the household ran smoothly. Crunniuc was a rich man.

BELOW: In Celtic mythology stones have magical properties. The ancient Irish erected stones, such as the Garrane Standing Stones, to mark sacred spaces and boundaries. OPPOSITE: Lismore Castle peeks through the trees in Co. Waterford.

The day of the Ulster fair arrived. Everyone in Ulster went to the fair, except Crunniuc's woman, for she was heavy with child. Crunniuc went, dressed in the beautiful clothes the woman had made him. He felt good.

"Take care while at the fair," the woman said. "Do not boast of your blessings or grow careless in your talk."

"That isn't likely," said Crunniuc.

At the fair, horse races were held to test the mettle of the horses and the skill of the chariot drivers. The king's horse and chariot sped past all comers, winning easily.

"There's not a horse in Ireland that can beat the king's horse," said one man.

"Indeed," said another. "There is not anyone or anything in Ireland that can beat the king's horses."

"Quite so," said yet another. "I would wager not even the steeds of the Sídh could beat the king's horses."

Crunniuc could not ignore the challenge.

"That is not so," said Crunniuc. "It is only because the horses belong to the king that they have won."

"That is a lie," said one man.

"A damnable lie," said another.

"The king will hear of this slur," said yet another.

Crunniuc scoffed. "My wife, even though she is nine months with child, could beat the king's horses."

The king was told of Crunniuc's boast, and he had Crunniuc seized and brought before him. The king sent a messenger for Crunniuc's wife.

"I am heavy with child," said Crunniuc's wife. "I cannot go and free him now."

"He will die for his false boast if you do not come," said the king's messenger.

The woman gathered her things and followed the king's messenger. As she neared the fairgrounds, her water broke and her birth pangs came upon her.

"Help me!" she called to the crowd. "Wait until my children are born. You were all born of women! Have pity!"

The crowd wasn't moved.

"A curse on you, then," the woman said. "A curse on all Ulster!"

"What is your name?" the king asked.

"I am Macha," said the woman. "My name and that of my children will name this place for the ignoble deed you do here today."

Then Macha raced the king's chariot and won. As the chariot reached the end of the racing field, Macha gave birth to twins beside it. As she delivered her son and daughter, Macha screamed out, "May you all suffer the pangs of birth when you are in your greatest difficulty!"

From that time, for nine generations, the men of Ulster were so cursed that whenever they faced a great foe, they were doubled over with the pain of childbirth. From that day, too, the place of the fair of Ulster was called Emain Macha, the Twins of Macha. Only three classes of people were free from Macha's curse: the young boys of Ulster, the women of Ulster, and CuChulainn, the hero of Ulster.

Macha left Crunniuc as she had found him—living alone in a wild place with nothing of value. He was not worthy of her affection.

PART 2

THE ULSTER CYCLE

he Ulster Cycle includes stories about the rule of King Conchobor and his aristocratic Red Branch warriors, chief of whom is CúChulainn. The central story of the cycle is "The Táin Bó Cúailnge," or "The Cattle Raid of Cooley." This prose epic is the oldest vernacular epic in Western literature. It is the story of the attack of the forces of Queen Medb (MEHTH-iv) upon the men of Ulster. Medb and her men attack because she wants to regain ownership of the Brown Bull of Cooley.

Medb's curse comes true (see "The Twins of Macha"), and the men of Ulster, facing the invading forces of Queen Medb, are stricken with labor pangs. Only CúChulainn faces the Connachtmen. He is a mere seventeen years old, but he holds the invaders at bay until the Ulstermen's pangs have passed.

The stories of the Ulster Cycle describe a Celtic warrior society very much like the one Caesar describes. The warriors use chariots, but not as battle cars. The charioteers drive the warriors to the battle-field, where the warriors dismount and fight hand-to-hand. These warriors are headhunters, taking the heads of men who fall before them in battle as trophies. The head is imbued with power, and capturing the head of a fallen enemy gives the victor his power (see "The Destruction of Da Derga's Hostel").

Even though the stories in the Ulster Cycle depict a masculine warrior society, there is an undercurrent of a matrilineal pre-Celtic culture. Sons are put out to fosterage, for example, generally to the mother's sister. Mother's brothers also assume responsibility for rearing these fostered sons.

There are also a number of strong female characters in the Ulster Cycle. Queen Medb is just one of the many warrior women depicted. Medb is a goddess. She chooses husbands for a year and a day. She offers herself and her daughter Finnabair to men in order to get her way. Her menstrual blood creates rivers and valleys. Throughout these stories, women act as charioteers, trainers of warriors, leaders in battle, and, in many instances, instigators of action. The women in the Ulster Cycle are not passive. Even Derdriu, the Lady of Sorrows, takes control of her destiny, in spite of the best-laid plans of King Conchobor. "The Exile of the Sons of Uisliu," which is really Derdriu's story, is akin to classical Greek tales in its tragic elements—the heroine takes her own life rather than submit to Conchobor.

In a further parallel between the Irish stories and the Greek, King Conchobor is reminiscent of Homer's wily Odysseus. Conchobor's devious mind is part of his genetic makeup. His mother, Nes, is a worthy political strategist, securing the throne for her son from Fergus by bartering her sexual favors and through thievery and bribery. Conchobor learns well from his mother. Although he brings great prosperity to Ulster, Conchobor is not a man of his word. He offers Derdriu and her lover, Noisiu, safe passage, for example, but coerces another man into killing Noisiu and his brothers. It is this outrage, not the loss of the throne, that drives the great Ulster champion (and former king) Fergus over to the Connacht side in the battle between Connacht and Ulster over the Brown Bull of Cooley.

CúChulainn, the young hero of the Ulster Cycle and the son of Lug of the Tuatha Dé Danaan, also has qualities like those of Greek heroes. He, like Achilles, chooses a short but illustrious life.

The Birth of Conchobor

King Eochaid of Emain Macha had a daughter, Nes. Nes was very beautiful and extremely headstrong. One fine, sunny day she sat with fifty of her serving women on the Plain of Macha, enjoying the beauty of the day. She watched as a tall, dark-haired man approached. By his dress, she knew him to be a druid—one who sees the future and talks to unseen spirits.

"What is the hour good for?" Nes asked the druid, rather saucily.

He looked at her, his dark eyes atwinkle. "For begetting a king, my queen," he said.

This made Nes curious. "Is that really true?" she asked.

"By the gods that my people swear by, it is true," the druid said. "A son conceived at this very hour will be heard of in Ireland forever."

Nes looked around the Plain of Macha. There were no other men about.

"It will have to be you then," Nes said. "Come."

She led the druid inside the walls with her. They lay together and she conceived a son. When the boy was born, Nes took her son to the druid. The druid accepted the boy as his and named the child Conchobor, Cathbad the druid's son.

After the boy was born, Nes lived by herself as she had before, but the king, Fergus mac Roich, wooed her.

"Will you marry me?" Fergus asked.

"What do I get in return?" Nes asked.

"Whatever you desire," said Fergus. "Name your bride price and I will pay it."

"Give my son the kingship for a year," said Nes. "Then the people will call his son the son of a king."

"That's reasonable," said the people of the kingdom when Fergus brought the matter before them. "After all, the boy will be king in name only. We'll know that Fergus is really the king."

Fergus agreed to the arrangement, and Nes slept with him. She managed her son's kingship, as he was too young. She worked through Conchobor's foster parents.

"Take all the wealth from half of the people," Nes advised. "Give it to the other half." She spent her own gold and silver liberally among her personal guards.

At the end of the year, Fergus demanded the kingship back from the boy, Conchobor.

"We'll have to think about this," said the people of Ulster. "Things have been good with young Conchobor as king."

The people voted on the kingship and it was decided.

"What King Fergus has sold, let it stay sold," said the people. "Conchobor will remain as king."

The son of Nes and the druid Cathbad, thus became king of Ulster. The men of Ulster so respected Conchobor that to him they gave the right of first night. Every man, newly married, gave his bride to Conchobor the first night. Each man that Conchobor visited provided a bed and his wife. In return, Conchobor gave only well-thought-out judgments so that the crops and herds were plentiful. Conchobor was kept from harm by hardy warriors who went into battle before him.

Conchobor gathered the best warriors to court. Even young boys dreamt of joining the boy-troop at Emain Macha.

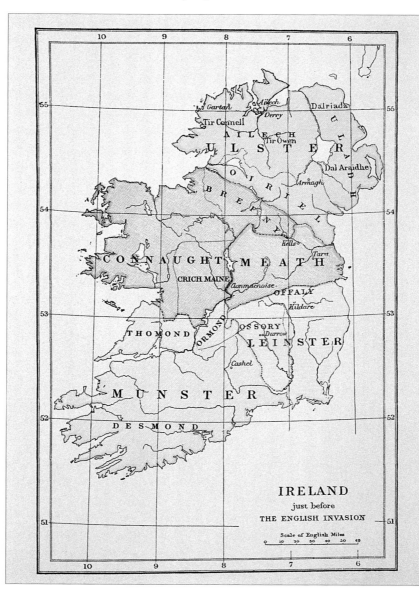

BELOW: Ireland's traditional provinces were Ulster, Leinster, Munster, and Connacht. The fifth, Meath, was the sacred boundary where the four met. OPPOSITE: The beautiful Nes lay with the druid Cathbad. Their child, Conchobor, was destined for greatness.

IRELAND
just before
THE ENGLISH INVASION

Scale of English Miles

The Birth and Boyhood Deeds of CúChulainn

One day as King Conchobor and his warriors were at Emain Macha, a great flock of birds descended on the green, stripping it of vegetation. They pulled up plants and even the grass by the roots. This desecration of Emain Macha angered the men of Ulster.

"Prepare the chariots," shouted King Conchobor. The people of Ulster prepared to force the birds out.

Nine chariots were brought forward. Deichtine, the king's sister, served as his charioteer. Conchobor and his warriors chased the flock, but as the chariots approached, the birds took flight. Conchobor and his warriors could not get within spear shot, yet they pursued the birds across the Plain of Macha and through the mountain pass of Sliab Fuait (SHLEE-av FOO-at). The birds led Conchobor and his warriors to Brug na Bóinne.

Night overtook them there and snow began to fall.

"Unyoke your chariots," ordered Conchobor. "Look for shelter." Two of Conchobor's warriors, Conall and Bricriu, scoured the countryside, looking for the light of a warm fire. They came across a newly built house of wood. The couple of the house welcomed the travelers and told them to bring their companions. The two warriors returned to their hunting party.

"There is a house nearby," said Conall to Conchobor, "but we had best take our own food. The servings will be sparse there."

"So be it," said Conchobor.

BELOW: With imagination, an old cottage becomes the mysterious house that Conchobor and his warriors found in the mist. OPPOSITE: In Irish mythology, the birds of the Sidh stripped the countryside bare of vegetation, creating a stark landscape.

The hunting party crowded into the small enclosure. It didn't take long before the Ulstermen found the couple's hidden storeroom and had served themselves. Soon Conchobor and his warriors were singing with drink. The man's wife did not serve them, as was custom.

"Where is your wife, good host?" asked King Conchobor.

"In truth," said the man of the house, "she is in her birth pangs at this very moment in the storeroom."

Deichtine immediately went into the storeroom to help the woman of the house with the birthing. At the very instant that the woman gave birth to a son, a mare at the door of the house had twin foals. Conchobor gave the foals to the newborn infant as a gift. The Ulstermen took charge of the baby boy, giving him to Deichtine to be nursed. Then all slept.

In the morning, the Ulster warriors awoke to find themselves alone. The house and the man and woman had disappeared, leaving only the infant behind. The Ulstermen left the place, taking the baby with them. Upon reaching Emain Macha, they voted to give the baby to Deichtine for fostering.

Deichtine raised him until he was a boy, but he became sick and died. Deichtine keened for him and

BELOW: *The country-side of Kerry is the body of the goddess Anu (also known as Danu). Ireland is always a woman.*

48

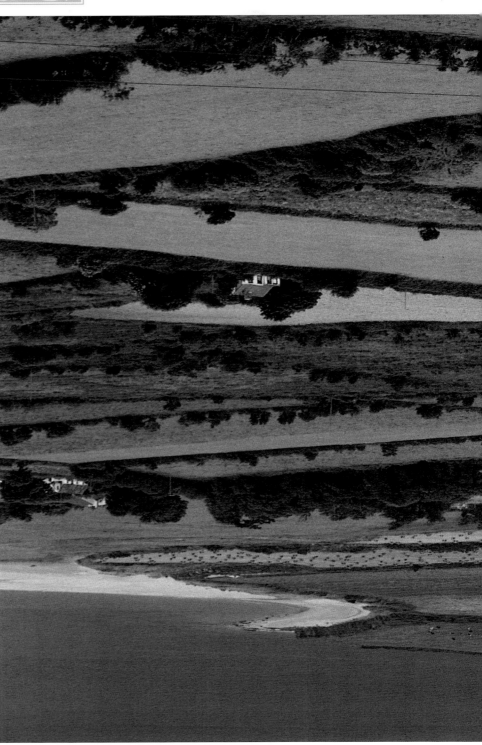

spent long hours mourning at his grave. When she returned home, she was thirsty and asked for a drink. Unknowingly, as she lifted the cup to her lips, Deichtine swallowed a small creature with the drink. That night she dreamt a strange dream.

A beautiful man of the Sídh came to her in her dream.

"You will bear my son," said the man. "I am the man from the Brug; I am Lug of the Long Arm. I brought you there so that you would bear my son. The boy that you raised was mine. I have planted him in your womb this time. You will call him Sétanta. The foals are to be raised with the boy that I have given you."

Deichtine grew heavy with child and people gossiped.

"Who is the father of Deichtine's child?" they wondered.

"Well, she was alone in the Brug with her brother, Conchobor."

"Who knows what he did in his drunkenness," said another suggested one.

Conchobor arranged a marriage for Deichtine with Sualdam, a great warrior and nobleman, hoping to stop the gossip among the Ulstermen. But Deichtine was ashamed of going pregnant to her marriage bed. She destroyed the child she carried, and so went whole to her new husband. However, she was soon with child again. She named the son she bore Sétanta, as Lug of the Long Arm had instructed her to in her dream. The infant was given to Finnchaem (FINN-him), another sister of Conchobor's, and her husband, Amargin (AV-ar-ghin), for fostering at Murtheimne (mur-THEV-nuh) Plain.

Sétanta grew quickly because he was the son of Lug. By the age of seven he was eager to join the boy-troop of Conchobor at Emain Macha. Sétanta had heard often of the boy-troop of which King Conchobor was so proud, and he begged his foster mother, Finnchaem, to let him join.

"You are not yet old enough," said Finnchaem. "You must wait for an Ulster warrior to accompany you."

"That will take too long," Sétanta complained. "Just point me the way to Emain Macha. I can find it by myself."

"It is a long way and the road is hard," said Finnchaem. "You must go through Slíab Fúait to the north."

"I will try," said Sétanta.

He left his foster parents' home on Murtheimne Plain, carrying a toy shield and javelin, and a hurling stick and ball. As he walked, he tossed his javelin and ran to catch it before it hit the ground. So engrossed was he in his game that he covered the ground between Murtheimne Plain and Emain Macha quickly. At last he came upon Conchobor's boy-troop at Emain Macha, but he didn't know the customs of the country, for no Ulster warrior accompanied him. It was the rule that anyone approaching the boy-troop had to ask for a promise of safety from the troop. Sétanta did not know that he defied custom. He kept on moving toward the boy-troop.

"Stop, stranger," the boys yelled at him.

Sétanta continued on. The boys threw their javelins at him. He stopped them all with his toy shield. The boys then drove their hurling balls at him, but Sétanta stopped them with his chest. With no weapons remaining save their hurling sticks, the boys threw those at Sétanta, but he dodged all the sticks. The poor reception from the boy-troop consumed Sétanta with a warrior's anger.

All the hair on his head stood on end and looked like it was afire. With one eye squinted and nearly closed, and the other nearly popping out of his head, Sétanta bared his teeth and charged the boys. He knocked a third of them down as they ran for the gates of Emain Macha. Nine boys fled into King Conchobor's room, where the king sat playing chess with Fergus. Sétanta raced after the fleeing boys, who in their haste knocked over the chessboard. King Conchobor caught Sétanta by the arm.

"What is this?" Conchobor demanded. "Why do you mistreat my boy-troop?"

"I did nothing wrong," Sétanta replied. "I was merely seeking their company."

"What is your name, boy?" asked Conchobor.

"I am Sétanta, the son of Sualdam and your sister Deichtine," the boy answered.

"Why didn't you put yourself under the boys' protection?" Conchobor asked.

"I knew nothing of this," said Sétanta. "I ask your protection from the boys, my king."

"You have it," said Conchobor. And from then on Sétanta joined the boy-troop in their games on the playing field. One day not long thereafter, King Conchobor was invited to Culann's house. Culann was a famous smith, but he didn't have a large house. He asked the king to bring only a small party. Conchobor agreed to take only his fifty best warriors. On his way to Culann's, Conchobor stopped at the playing field to watch the boy-troop practice their war maneuvers. Sétanta played ball against the entire boy-troop. They couldn't score against him, yet he drove the ball past them easily. Conchobor was impressed.

"Nephew," said Conchobor, "I am invited to Culann the smith's for dinner. He has asked that I bring my best warriors. Come with us to the feast."

"Thank you for the invitation, Uncle," said Sétanta. "By your leave, my king, I haven't had my fill of play yet. I will come later."

BELOW: The four-foot-high Turoe Stone, Co. Galway, dates from the first wave of Celtic immigration to Ireland. OPPOSITE: Palm trees grace the Johnston Castle grounds, Co. Wexford. Irish sailors brought the palms to Ireland.

"As you wish," said Conchobor.

Culann the smith met King Conchobor and his fifty warriors and brought them into his house, which was warm with welcoming fires and filled with the smells of roasting pig and ale.

"Is anyone coming late?" asked Culann.

"No," responded the king, forgetting that young Sétanta would be following. At this, Culann directed his steward to close the doors and to let loose the hound that guarded the home.

As dusk descended, Sétanta hurried toward the home of Culann the smith, traveling as before, throwing his javelin into the air and catching it before it fell. But his playful mood was shattered when Culann's watchdog attacked him just outside the house. Sétanta threw his javelin and other toys aside. He grabbed the hound around the neck with both hands and smashed it against a stone pillar until it died.

Conchobor's men rushed from the house with a great shout and hoisted Sétanta onto their shoulders.

"Well done, young warrior," said Fergus.

"Well done, my nephew," said Conchobor.

Only Culann the smith was silent. "I am happy that you were not injured, young warrior," said Culann. "But your triumph has cost me the champion of my house. Who will protect me and mine?"

"I will take his place," said Sétanta. "Until a pup from the same bitch can be raised to be your security, I will protect you and your herds."

"That is acceptable," said Culann the smith.

So it was that Sétanta became CúChulainn, a name meaning the hound (cu) of Culann the smith. From that time on it was taboo for CuChulainn to eat the flesh of a dog, for he now bore the name of a dog.

The Exile of the Sons of Uisliu

One evening, King Conchobor and his men sat eating and drinking in the house of the king's storyteller, Fedlimid (FEH-lim-ih). The storyteller's wife was an excellent hostess, making sure that no one's cup was empty and that all had plenty to eat. However, she moved slowly through the crowded hall, being nearly ready to deliver the child she bore. At the end of the evening, the king and his men retired to their sleeping couches, while the storyteller's wife oversaw the cleaning of the great hall. When she finally made her way to her bed, there came a terrible scream from within her womb.

The warriors of Ulster sprang from their beds and grabbed their weapons, thinking an enemy was at hand. There was much noise and confusion.

"Quiet," yelled Cathbad the druid. "Quiet. We will soon sort this out."

He motioned to the woman to come forward.

"What was that horrible noise?" asked her husband.

"I swear that I do not know," she answered. She turned to the druid, "Do you know what this portent means, druid?"

Cathbad placed his hand on the woman's swollen belly. "A woman with golden hair, green eyes of great beauty, cheeks like foxglove, teeth whiter than snow, and lips of Parthian red cried out from your womb," Cathbad said. "Many Ulster chariot-warriors will fight for her. Heroes will vie for her. Many men will die for her."

The baby wriggled under the druid's hand. "Yes, there is a girl there," Cathbad said. "Her name shall be Derdriu. She will bring evil."

The girl was born that night. The Ulster warriors murmured among themselves.

"What are you whispering about?" demanded King Conchobor.

"My king, let us kill this girl child," said a warrior, "lest she bring death and destruction upon us."

"No," said Conchobor. "She will be taken from here and raised for me. I will keep her for myself."

Conchobor sent the girl away from Emain Macha. No one was allowed to see her except her foster father and mother and Leborcham, a satirist who was allowed to go anywhere he wanted because the people feared his curses.

The years passed and Derdriu did indeed grow into a beautiful young woman, as the druid had predicted. One winter day she stood talking with Leborcham on the

BELOW: Noisiu and his brothers sought to keep Derdriu safe from the prying eyes of lustful men by building special houses.
OPPOSITE: Derdriu desired a man with fair skin, raven hair, and ruddy cheeks. She found him in Noisiu.

THE ULSTER CYCLE

ramparts of her foster parents' fortress. They watched as her foster father killed a milk-fed calf for Deirdriu's dinner. A black crow lit on the white snow and greedily drank the scarlet-stained, steaming snow.

"I could desire a man like that," Deirdriu said.

"What do you mean?" asked the satirist.

"I could desire a man with raven hair, ruddy cheeks, and fair skin," Deirdriu answered.

"Lucky for you," said Leborcham, who enjoyed creating havoc, "that I know where you can find just such a man."

"Where?" teased Deirdriu.

"Close by," said Leborcham. "If you listen carefully, you can hear him chanting now."

Deirdriu listened to the wind wafting from Emain Macha. A beautiful voice carried on the wind, but she couldn't make out the words.

"Whose voice is that?" Deirdriu asked.

"The voice belongs to Noisiu, Uisliu's son," said Leborcham. "The sons of Uisliu are famous for their chanting. Did you know that any human who hears Noisiu or his brothers chanting is filled with peace and music?"

Deirdriu shook her head. "This cannot be," she said. "I am not filled with peace upon hearing the voice of Noisiu. I am filled with a desire to see this warrior."

"That cannot be," said Leborcham. "King Conchobor has decreed that you are to be his. It would be an evil thing to go against the king's wishes. You would also bring harm to Ulster, for the voices of Noisiu and his brothers cause the cows of Ulster to give two-thirds more milk."

"Maybe you are right," said Deirdriu, but she looked wistfully toward Emain Macha.

Leborcham took his leave. Deirdriu looked to see that no one watched her and fled her foster parents' home, following the beautiful voice she heard in the wind. She found Noisiu near Emain, chanting by himself. He was beautiful—raven hair, ruddy cheeks, fair skin, and a warrior's build. Deirdriu pretended she didn't know who he was and walked past him.

"That is a fine heifer going by," said Noisiu.

"The heifers get big where there are no bulls," responded Deirdriu, turning back to look at him.

Noisiu recognized her then. "You have the bull of this province to yourself. The king of Ulster will take you for his wife," said Noisiu.

BELOW: The Celtic cross graphically merges the ancient beliefs regarding the sacredness of the eternal round with Christianity's cross.

OPPOSITE: O'Brien's lighthouse keeps vigil at the very edge of Europe—Ireland's Cliffs of Moher, Co. Clare.

"Between the two of you," said Deirdriu, "I'd pick the young bull."

"That cannot be," said Noisiu. "Cathbad the druid foresaw evil should anyone possess you save the king."

"Are you rejecting me?" Deirdriu asked.

"I am," said Noisiu.

Deirdriu rushed at Noisiu, grabbed him by both his ears, and threw her legs around his waist, clinging to him.

"You will be shamed if you don't take me with you," she said.

Noisiu tried to loosen her arms from around his neck. "Leave me alone," he said.

"You will do it," she said, binding him with her words.

"No," cried Noisiu. His brothers came running then, seeking to know what had frightened him. His cry had alarmed the warriors of Ulster at Emain Macha as well, and they rushed to the Plain of Emain with their swords drawn.

"What's wrong?" asked Noisiu's older brother.

Noisiu told them what Deirdriu had done.

"Evil will come of this," said Noisiu's younger brother. "No one will believe that you rejected her."

"He's right," said the older brother. "We will have to flee, and we will have to take her with us."

Noisiu, his two brothers, and their retinues left Emain Macha that night for fear of Conchobor and his warriors. They took Deirdriu with them. They wandered Ireland, but found no peace, for Conchobor tried often to destroy them. Finally, the group fled to Scotland. They settled in a barren place, but the hunting was poor. Driven by hunger, they resorted to stealing cattle, which earned them the enmity of the Scottish people. Finding no peace in any quarter, Noisiu and his brothers went to the king of Scotland and asked for his protection. The king agreed to help them, and hired Noisiu and his two brothers and their retinues as mercenaries.

"This is good," said Noisiu's older brother. "At last we have some peace."

Noisiu nodded agreement.

"But not for long," said Noisiu's younger brother. "We will have no peace if anyone looks on Deirdriu, for all who do will desire her."

"You are right," said Noisiu. "If the Scottish king should see her, there will be bloodshed. What shall we do?"

"We will build our houses so that no one can look in," said Noisiu's older brother. "We will turn our three houses to face each other, their backs to the world."

The Ulster Cycle

But the houses themselves aroused curiosity. Many wondered what Noisiu and his brothers sought to hide. The Scottish king sent his steward to spy on the brothers and to uncover their secret. One night, as everyone slept, the steward crept into the compound and peered into Noisiu's house. He saw Derdriu, the most beautiful woman in the world, asleep beside Noisiu. He hurried to his king to make his report.

"I have never seen a woman worthy of you until today," he said to the king. "You must kill Noisiu and take this woman for your own."

"I have given this man and his brothers my protection," said the king. "It would be against the laws of hospitality to harm him. But I can woo the lady and let her make her own choice."

Every day the Scottish king sent his steward to Derdriu after Noisiu and his brothers had left for the day.

"Lady," said the steward, "my master, the king of Scotland, desires to sleep with you. Will you consent?"

"I have chosen Noisiu," said Derdriu.

Each night, when Noisiu and his brothers returned, Derdriu would tell them of the steward's visit. The king grew impatient with Derdriu's replies. He sent Noisiu and his brothers on the most danger-ous missions, hoping that a foe might accomplish what he dared not do—the killing of the brothers. But the brothers were formidable in battle and overcame all their opponents. At last, the king despaired of ever achieving his goal.

"Steward," he said, "tell the maid that unless she sleeps with me, I will kill her beloved Noisiu and his brothers. Perhaps she will choose the better course."

The steward gave the message to Derdriu, who repeated it to Noisiu that evening.

"We must flee," said Noisiu's older brother.

"But we cannot return to Ireland because of this woman," said Noisiu's younger brother.

"Then we will remain between the two," said Noisiu. "There is a safe island in the sea between Scotland and Ireland. We will take refuge there."

The tale of Noisiu and his brothers reached Conchobor's court.

"It would be a great shame on Ireland if the Scottish king were to kill Noisiu and his two brothers," said the Ulstermen. "They are of us. We must rescue them."

"You are right," said Conchobor. "It would be a great dishonor to allow the Scots to kill Ulstermen."

The very next day, King Conchobor sent a messenger carrying his promise that he would give safe conduct to Emain Macha for the exiled band.

LEFT: Boys, descen-dants of the boy-troops of CuChulainn's time, still play on the lakeshore.

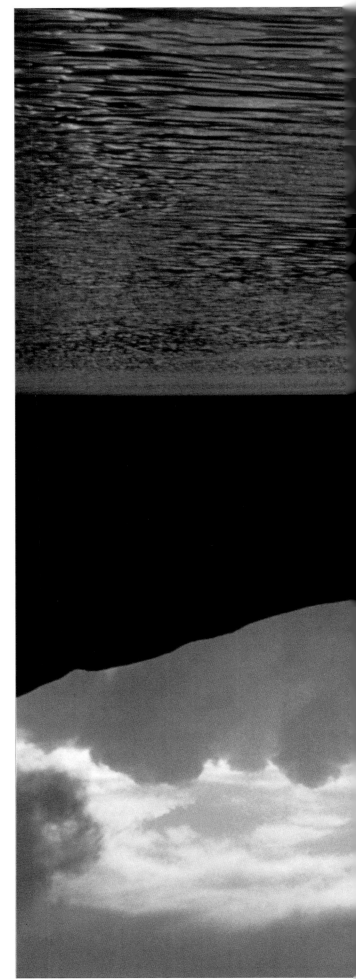

"We will come to Emain Macha," said Noisiu, "But only on one condition."

"Name it," said the messenger.

"We will come to Emain Macha only if three warriors we respect come to take us there," said Noisiu. "Namely, Fergus, Dubthach, and Conchobor's own son, Cormac."

"This will be done," replied the messenger.

As agreed, Conchobor sent Fergus, Dubthach, and his own son, Cormac, to lead Noisiu and his brothers to Emain Macha, but he plotted against them in secret. He made a pact with Eogan, king of Fernmag, with whom he had been at war. Eogan, whose power was far less than Conchobor's, sought to make peace with the high king, and here Conchobor saw an opportunity to take out his revenge on Noisiu.

"You seek peace, Eogan," said Conchobor. "That is good. But what does peace bring me? I can defeat you at any time, which will help build my reputation for being strong. Peace, therefore, is in your best interest, but I gain nothing."

"What can I give you, King Conchobor, that you do not already possess?" asked Eogan. "Perhaps, though, there is a service that I can perform that no one else can."

"You speak wisely," said Conchobor. "Indeed, I have just such a task to be completed."

"Tell me, King Conchobor," said Eogan. "And I will do it."

"I have given my word to Noisiu and his brothers that I will not harm them," said Conchobor. "But I do not want them to live."

"I will see to it," said Eogan.

Fergus, Dubthach, and Cormac brought the doomed exiles closer to Emain Macha even as Conchobor and Eogan plotted against them. Fergus, however, had to leave the group when an ale feast was proclaimed. Because of a taboo on him, Fergus was obligated to attend all ale feasts; Conchobor knew that Fergus would keep his oath and go, and knew that the group would be weakened without him.

"I must go to this ale feast," said Fergus to Noisiu. "I have sworn an oath to the gods my people swear by. I cannot break my vow."

"A vow must be kept," said Noisiu.

"Stay here," said Fergus. "I will return soon, and we can resume our journey to Emain Macha."

"My brothers and I have also sworn an oath," said Noisiu. "We have sworn that we will not eat until we have reached Emain Macha and been reconciled with King Conchobor."

"A vow must be kept," said Fergus. "I will leave you in good hands. My own son, Fiacha, will lead you the rest of the way."

The next day, Noisiu, his brothers, and their retinues prepared to enter the green in front of Emain Macha. The women of Emain stood

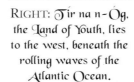

RIGHT: Tír na n-Óg, the Land of Youth, lies to the west, beneath the rolling waves of the Atlantic Ocean.

on the ramparts, watching. As Noisiu and his brothers came into the green, they were surrounded by Eogan and his men, Conchobor's henchmen. Fergus' son, Fiacha, stood shoulder to shoulder with Noisiu. When Eogan was within spear-throwing distance, he launched a great spear that went through Noisiu with such force that it broke his back.

Fiacha threw his arms around Noisiu, pulled him to the ground, and threw himself across Noisiu's body in a vain attempt to protect him. Eogan thrust his spear again, killing them both.

Slaughter broke out across the plain. Derdriu was captured and taken to Conchobor, her hands bound behind her.

Some men escaped the ambush and made their way to Fergus.

"Fergus," said the first one. "I bring terrible news. Death and betrayal."

"Tell me," said Fergus.

"Conchobor has betrayed his oath," said the second.

"Conchobor has given the killing of Noisiu and his brothers to Eogan," said a third.

"My son, Fiacha, will see that Conchobor keeps his word," said Fergus.

"Alas," cried the first. "Your son, Fiacha, has kept his oath, but Conchobor's treachery has taken his life."

"Eogan will die for killing my son. Conchobor will suffer for his treachery," vowed Fergus.

Dubthach and Cormac joined Fergus, and they marched on Emain Macha. There was great slaughter on the Plain of Emain as Fergus exacted his revenge. Three hundred men fell in battle, and Dubthach massacred all the girls of Ulster in the night. Fergus burned Emain Macha to the ground.

At the king's castle, Conchobor kept Derdriu to himself. For a year, she never smiled, ate, or slept. She sat with her head to her knees. She would not listen to music or Conchobor's sweet words.

"Noisiu's voice was sweet," Derdriu said. "There is no more sweetness in the world."

ABOVE: Christianity came to Ireland in the sixth century. Tradition holds that Saint Patrick, a Christian and former slave, converted the country. OPPOSITE: The Normans and the English divided Ireland. They ruled from from castle strongholds, such as Clifden Castle, Co. Galway.

"Is there nothing I can give you," said Conchobor, "that will make you look upon me the way you did Noisiu?"

"I cannot see you," said Derdriu. "I see Noisiu, dressing in the dim dawning light at the edge of the forest."

"What can I say that will ease your hatred of me?" asked King Conchobor.

"Noisiu's voice was sweet, chanting in the dark forests," said Derdriu. "But you have taken his voice from the world."

"If I cannot please you, you can still please me," said Conchobor. "Put on your finest, as you did for Noisiu."

"I no longer paint my fingernails. Why should I? I cannot eat. I cannot sleep," said Derdriu. "You have taken the thing I most loved in the world, Conchobor. Why should I please you?"

"You go too far," Conchobor said.

Derdriu looked at her hands and said nothing. She turned away.

"Enough, woman," said Conchobor. "What do you hate the most?"

"You," said Derdriu. "And Eogan, the man who killed my love."

"Fine," said Conchobor. "Go and live with Eogan for a year, then. He, too, can enjoy your company. Maybe after spending time with Eogan, you will grow to appreciate me more."

"Neither of you will ever possess me," said Derdriu. "I swear it."

"We shall see," said Conchobor.

The next day Eogan took her in his chariot and left Emain Macha. As the chariot pulled away, Derdriu saw a big block of stone rise up in front. She leaned over the side of the chariot and let her head be driven against the stone, and in this way she died.

Fergus and Dubthach with their households fled to Connacht and joined those who served King Ailill and Queen Medb. From Connacht they waged war on Ulster for sixteen years.

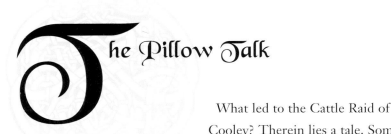

The Pillow Talk

What led to the Cattle Raid of Cooley? Therein lies a tale. Some say it was bad blood between two kings of the Sídh and a competition that got out of hand. Others say it was competition and envy between Ailill and Medb in their marriage bed. Or perhaps it was because Ailill and Medb saw weakness in the Ulstermen after Conchobor's ignoble deed, the treacherous killing of Noisiu and his two brothers. Conchobor's own son, Cormac, joined Fergus in exile in Connacht, and from Connacht the Ulstermen in exile waged war on Conchobor. Whatever the reason, the cattle raid was ill-fated. Much misery resulted from the search for the great Brown Bull of Cooley and the desire to possess him.

There were actually two bulls: the White and the Brown. The two bulls became enchanted because of a dispute between two kings. The king of the Sídh in Connacht was at odds with the king of the Sídh in Munster. Each king had a keeper of pigs, a magician who could change into any shape he chose. These magicians were friends, even though their employers were always at blows. They were such good friends that they often herded their pigs together, for they enjoyed one another's company.

"Greetings," said the one to the other, after a fairly long absence. "It's good to see you."

"Hello to you," said the other. "I am glad of the welcome. With the competition between our two kings, I didn't know if you would be glad to see me."

"What do the doings of our kings have to do with us?" said the first.

"Well said," said the second. "I am tired of listening to all the ill-tempered talk of boasting men seeking to create a competition between us."

BELOW: The houses Noisiu and his brothers built turned their backs to the world, like this Iron-Age ring fort at Staigue, Co. Kerry. OPPOSITE: The two magicians underwent many transformations before becoming the great Brown Bull of Cooley and the White Bull.

"What talk is that?" asked the first.

"Oh, the troublemakers seek to stir up bad blood between us with their evil tongues," said the second. "Surely, you've heard them?"

"What do they say?" asked the first.

"Such talk as, 'Your power is greater than mine,'" said the second.

"Surely this isn't the boasting talk you spoke of," said the first.

"What do you mean by that?" asked the second.

"They speak the truth, do they not?" asked the first.

"That's something we can put to the test," said the second.

"A wager?" asked the first.

"A wager," said the second.

"I'll wager that I can cast a spell on your pigs so that they may eat acorns galore, but they won't put on any fat. They will be bags of bones even though they eat their fill," said the first.

"You're on," said the second.

The first magician put a spell on the second magician's pigs so that they grew skinnier and skinnier even though they ate their fill. When it came time for the second magician to return to Connacht, his pigs were walking skeletons. His countrymen laughed.

"We told you the Munster magician had greater skill than you," they said.

The Connacht magician brooded for a year until the Munster magician brought his pigs to Connacht, and then he successfully put the same curse on the Munster pigs.

"They have the same powers," said the Connachtmen.

This angered the king of the Connacht Sídh, for he wanted to have the most powerful magician. So he fired his pigkeeper magician. The king of the Munster Sídh did the same. "What is the point of having a magician if his powers are equally met?" the Sídh kings asked.

This led to enmity between the two magicians. Each tried to outdo the other. One year they became hawks, chasing and clawing at one another. The following year they became great eels, each trying to devour the other. The third year they became great stags and

destroyed one another's deer herds and dwellings. The fourth year they were great warriors and hacked each other to pieces. They spent the next year as spirits. The sixth year they became dragons and buried each other in mounds of snow. Finally, in the seventh year, they became maggots in two of the sacred springs of Ireland. A cow in Munster drank one, and a cow in Connacht drank the other. Thus it was that the two magicians were born as bulls: the Brown Bull of Cooley and the White Bull of Ai.

But that was just the beginning of the strife that was to be. For one night, as they lay in bed together, Ailill smiled at Medb.

"Why do you smile at me?" asked Medb.

"I was just thinking how lucky you are," said Ailill, "to have me as a husband."

"Why does that make me lucky?" asked Medb.

"There aren't many women who are better off after they marry," said Ailill.

"And I'm better off?" said Medb.

"I've given you great wealth, and I keep your beautiful things from being carried off by your enemies."

"You think highly of yourself," said Medb. "You brought no more wealth into our marriage than I already possessed. I am, after all, the daughter of the high king of Ireland. My father gave me this province of Cruachan to rule as my own. What did your father give you in Leinster?"

"As a man and a warrior, I protect you from men who prey on the weakness of women," said Ailill. "You would have no wealth if I weren't here. It would all have been carried off by marauders."

Medb laughed. "Long before I met you, I dealt with such thievery myself. I led fifteen hundred foreign mercenaries and an equal number of freeborn natives into battle. But," said Medb, running her fingers through Ailill's hair, "I wouldn't have any other man as my mate, for we are much alike. If anyone shames you, he will answer to me, for I bought you with a wealth of wedding gifts."

"It remains that women aren't meant to rule," said Ailill.

"If we are equal in wealth and ability," asked Medb, "how can you say such a thing?"

"We aren't equal," Ailill told her. "My wealth is much greater than yours."

"It isn't," said Medb.

"It is," said Ailill.

And so it was that in the middle of the night they caused their servants to bring out and enumerate all their belongings. Each met wealth with wealth. If one had silver and gold, the other had silver and gold. If one had beautiful woolen garments, the other had beautiful

woolen garments. Their horse herds matched each other's. Their pig herds were equally fine. As the inventory was added up, Medb was found lacking in only one thing. Her fine bull, the White Bull of Ai, refusing to serve a woman, had wandered off and taken his place among Ailill's herd of cows. Medb was furious. She called for Mac Roth, her messenger.

"What is this, Mac Roth?" she roared. "How am I to match this fine bull?"

"I know where there is another," said Mac Roth. "There is the Brown Bull of Cooley in Ulster that is the equal of the White."

"Get him, Mac Roth," said Medb. "And I don't care how. Offer his owner anything. Even pasturage on my own Plain of Ai. If that

doesn't sway him, tell him he can also have my friendly thighs. And if he won't give the bull to me by asking, then you are to take it by force."

"As you wish, my queen," said Mac Roth.

So it was that Mac Roth went to Dáire, the man who possessed the Brown Bull of Cooley in Ulster, and asked to borrow the bull. Mac Roth told Dáire what Medb was willing to pay for the loan of the bull.

"You can have fifty heifers, pasturage on the Plain of Ai, and Medb's friendly thighs," said Mac Roth.

"You have a deal," said Dáire.

To celebrate, they drank together. By dawn they were tipsy.

"It's a good thing you agreed to loan the Brown Bull to Medb," said Mac Roth. "I like you. I would have hated to have to kill you for it. If you hadn't agreed to loan the bull, Medb would have had it by force."

"You mean, you would have tried to take it by force," said Dáire, laughing.

"It wouldn't have been that difficult," said Mac Roth.

At that Dáire jumped up, exclaiming, "It's only because I don't murder messengers or travelers that you are not dead for your pains." He challenged MacRoth, "Return to Medb and tell her to try to take the bull by force."

And that is just what Mac Roth did.

ABOVE: Ireland's bounty fed the pigs of the Sídh. From her woods, she provided oak mast to fatten the pigkeeper's herds.

THE ULSTER CYCLE

The Battle of the Bulls

Mac Roth wasted no time in returning to Medb and reporting that Daire refused to relinquish the Brown Bull of Cuailnge and that he had dared her to take it.

"Take it I will," said Medb.

She prepared for war. Ailill, her husband, joined her in the endeavor to capture the bull.

Fergus, the Ulster exile, agreed to join the expedition as well. Fergus still sought revenge for the death of his son and the stain on his honor brought about by Conchobor's treachery against Noisiu and his brothers. Also, Medb offered him her friendly thighs if he would join her army. So it was that Medb rallied the armies of Connacht and the Ulster exiles to take the Brown Bull of Cuailnge by force.

But the coming battle was clouded by evil omens. Fedelm, the prophetess, cried out.

"I see crimson; I see red!" she wailed.

But Medb dismissed the dismal wail by pointing out that any time warriors meet in battle there is blood and gore.

The armies marched toward Ulster, but again they were beset by an evil omen. They traveled countersunwise—from west to southeast to east.

When word of the Connacht warriors heading toward Ulster reached the Ulstermen, Macha's curse came upon the men of Ulster. She had cursed them for their callousness toward her when they had made her race against the king's chariot even though she was heavy with child. She had cursed them so that in their time of greatest need the warriors of Ulster would suffer the pangs of labor.

Only CúChulainn, who was still a boy, and his father were not affected, for Macha had not cursed boys and old men. Alone they faced the combined forces of Connacht and the Ulster exiles. CúChulainn challenged the best of the Connacht forces to single combat.

One by one, CúChulainn fought the heroes of Connacht and defeated them, but the many battles took their toll, and CúChulainn was greatly wounded by the time the labor pangs of the Ulstermen had passed and they could join the battle against Medb, Ailill, and the forces of Connacht.

Because of his wounds and of Fergus' great regard for the Ulster hero, CúChulainn secured Fergus' agreement not to come against him

in battle. Fergus and his men withdrew from the field to take up a defensive position at the rear of the battle. Medb and Ailill and their troops faced the fresh forces of the Ulstermen alone. There was a great battle, and the forces of Connacht had the worst of it.

Both sides then agreed to let the bulls themselves choose, and so the bulls came together on the Plain of Ai at a place that became known as Tarbga, the Place of the Bulls' Battle.

The Brown Bull stomped on the head of the White, impaling his foot on the White's horn. The two bulls stood that way for more than a day. At last, Fergus approached and hit the Brown Bull with a stick, saying, "Shame on you. How dare you dishonor your clan."

White Bull. He dropped the White Bull's shoulder blade at the Place of the Shoulder Blade. He dropped the White Bull's genitals at Áth Luain, the Place of the Genitals. At last, in Ulster, the Brown Bull died at an oak grove; hence the place was named the Oak Stand of the Bull.

"All is lost, Fergus," said Medb.

"That is usually what happens when men follow the rump of a misguided woman," said Fergus.

Medb gave her daughter, Finnabair, to CúChulainn as his wife, for he had spared Medb's life.

Ailill and Medb made peace with the Ulstermen, and there was peace in Ireland for seven years.

BELOW: The bulls' battled, carving and creating the landscape of Ireland. The bulls' sacrifice kept the land alive.

At that, the Brown Bull pulled back his foot, breaking his leg in the process, but the White Bull lost his horn. A great battle ensued.

The Brown Bull drove the White Bull before him, into the lake beside Cruachan, which churned and boiled as the bulls continued to struggle beneath the water. When the Brown Bull emerged from the waters a day and a night later, he carried pieces of the White Bull on his horns.

Fergus' men sought to kill the bull, but Fergus forbade it.

"Let him go where he will," said Fergus.

The Brown Bull left for his own land, the land of Ulster. Everywhere he traveled, he dropped pieces of the White Bull, and the people named each place for the

The Death of CúChulainn

Ailill and Medb made peace with the Ulstermen and returned to Connacht. There was peace for seven years after that. But foes of the Ulstermen came against them again, and CúChulainn read the signs of his approaching death. Fire and smoke filled Ulster. Weapons fell from their racks in the hall of his castle. As he dressed for battle, the brooch in his mantle fell to the floor. He stepped on it, piercing his foot, an evil omen.

CúChulainn had two horses, the twin foals presented to him by Conchobor upon his birth: the Gray and the Black of Macha. The Gray refused to be harnessed to the chariot.

"I cannot harness the Gray," said Loeg, CúChulainn's charioteer. "You will have to calm him yourself."

But when CúChulainn tried to harness the Gray himself, the horse turned its left side to him three times—another evil omen, for it was countersunwise.

BELOW: A prehistoric tomb made of undressed stones still stands at Carrowmore, Co. Sligo. OPPOSITE: Stones are sacred. Blarney Castle's stone gives the gift of oratory to all those who kiss it.

"How dare you dishonor me in this manner," said CúChulainn to the Gray. "Do you wish evil upon me?"

At this, the horse relented and let himself be harnessed.

CúChulainn turned his chariot toward the sun and rode past the walls of Emain Macha. The women of Emain Macha stood on the walls and keened for him, for they knew he would never return.

As CúChulainn rode to battle, he met three old women beside the road. They had roasted a dog on a spit over a rowan tree fire.

"Greetings, O CúChulainn," called out the first crone. "Come, visit with us."

"I will not," said CúChulainn. "I am forbidden by my taboos to stop."

"We have very little," said the second crone. "But we are glad to share."

"I cannot," said CúChulainn.

"It is because we offer only the flesh of a dog," said the third crone, accusingly. "You do not stop because we are poor and you are mighty."

Courtesy thus demanded that CúChulainn stop. He dismounted and joined their company. Although it was against a taboo of his to eat his namesake, he took the shank of dog that the first crone handed him. There was evil in the women, for when the crone handed him the dog

flesh, she did so with her left hand. CúChulainn received the flesh with his left hand, and at that very moment the strength left his arm.

CúChulainn left the women and headed into battle against his enemy, Erc. CúChulainn had killed the father of Erc, and Erc now sought revenge. With a sword that quickly grew bloody, CúChulainn attacked the ranks of Erc. The warriors stood shield to shield against him. But CúChulainn hacked off heads and arms, and left red bones scattered on the Plain of Murtheimne.

"Give me your spear," called a satirist. "I demand it."

"I cannot," said CúChulainn. "I need it more than you."

"You must. Custom dictates," said the satirist. "If you do not, I will curse you."

CúChulainn threw his spear at the satirist, piercing the man's head and killing nine others who stood beside him. Lugaid, an enemy warrior, picked up the spear and threw it back at CúChulainn. Lugaid knew that CúChulainn could only be destroyed by his own weapons. But the spear missed CúChulainn, striking and disemboweling his charioteer, Loeg.

CúChulainn pulled the spear out of Loeg and took the reins of the chariot himself.

"Give me your spear," called a second satirist. "I demand it."

"I will not," said CúChulainn.

"I will curse you," said the satirist.

CúChulainn again threw his spear, killing the second satirist and nine men beside him. Erc, CúChulainn's enemy, grabbed the spear and threw it back at CúChulainn. This time, it struck the Gray Horse of Macha. CúChulainn unharnessed the mortally wounded horse, which made its way to Sliab Fuait and died.

A third time, CúChulainn made his way to the battlefield.

"Give me your spear, CúChulainn," yelled a third satirist, "or I will curse you."

"I have kept one request today. I am not duty-bound to do more," said CúChulainn.

"The men of Ulster are stingy," said the satirist, "as are the men of your race."

CúChulainn threw his spear, killing the satirist and nine men beside him. Lugaid, the enemy warrior, picked up the spear and threw it at CúChulainn. This time, the spear pierced CúChulainn, disemboweling him. The frightened Black Horse of Macha pulled the reins from CúChulainn's hand and fled. Thus, CúChulainn was left alone on Murtheimne Plain, fatally wounded. His enemies surrounded him ready to finish him off.

"Before you kill me," said CúChulainn, "grant me permission to go to yonder lake to drink my fill."

"You have our permission," said Erc. "But you must return and face your doom."

"If I cannot return," said CúChulainn, "come get me."

CúChulainn wrapped his mantle around him to hold his bowels in place. He walked to the lake and washed himself. He drank his fill, and then turned his back to the lake. He walked to a nearby standing stone and fastened his girdle around it, binding himself to the rock, so he could die standing up. He held his sword in his right hand.

"I am ready," called CúChulainn to his enemies. Then he died.

His enemies surrounded him, but they didn't come close for fear of his warrior's prowess. He looked as though he still lived.

"It would be a shame not to take his head," said Lugaid. "After all, he took your father's head, did he not, Erc?"

The Morrígu and her two sisters, the three battle goddesses, the specters of the battlefield, came to CúChulainn then in the shape of carrion crows. They sat on his shoulder.

"He is dead," said Erc.

CúChulainn's enemies approached him. Lugaid pulled CúChulainn's hair to the side and cut off his head. As he did this, the sword in CúChulainn's right hand fell and cut off Lugaid's right hand. In retaliation, Erc cut CúChulainn's right hand off, and with

BELOW: *The monuments erected by the conquerors sink back into the Irish landscape. Ireland has been a melting pot throughout its history.*

CúChulainn's head and hand, Erc and his warriors made their way back to Tara. But CúChulainn was avenged. His foster brother, Conall, took Lugaid's head later that same day. There was much sorrow at Emain Macha that day, for CúChulainn was dead.

PART 3

The Fenian Cycle

Some scholars argue that Finn mac Cumhaill is another name for the Tuatha Dé Danann champion Lug of the Long Arm. Finn, after all, is a warrior and hunter without peer. Lug is always described as the bright one, Finn as the white one (indeed, Finn means "white" in Irish). As Lug destroyed his grandfather, Balor of the evil eye, Finn too defeats a one-eyed being. Finn's cycle of stories became increasingly popular starting in the twelfth century, a book deal later than material from the Ulster and Mythological cycles.

Finn's followers are called the fiana (FEE-nah). The fiana are a roving band of hunters and warriors. According to the stories, there are 150 men in the group. Each member brings to the group twenty-seven retainers. Members of the fiana are bound by conditions of service: to wit, they are not allowed to take material compensation; they must give valuables and meat to those in need; and they are not to run from nine or fewer warriors. Both the paternal and maternal sides of each fian's family have to give sureties that, should the fian be killed in battle, the family will not seek revenge. Vengeance belongs to the fiana. Members of the fiana were forbidden to seek redress from other members' families as well. Each member of the fiana also had to be a poet.

In addition to these requirements, would-be members of the fiana had to pass an initiation ceremony. The young warrior was placed waist-deep in a hole, with only a shield and hazel wand for protection. Nine members of the fiana then threw spears at him. If he were hurt, he could not be a fian. If he survived that test, the initiate would braid his hair and then flee through the woods, the fiana in hot pursuit. If he were overtaken or wounded, if he showed fear (signified by his weapons shaking in his hand), or if a strand of hair were displaced from his braid while he was running through the trees, the young man was not taken into the fiana. He also had to jump over a stick that was as high as his eyebrows, and to crawl under one as low as his knees. He had to be able to remove a thorn from his foot with a nail without slowing his pace. Then, and only then, could the young warrior be a fian.

There is an air of sadness in the Fenian Cycle. The most renowned love story of the Fenian Cycle, "The Pursuit of Diarmuid and Gráinne," dates to a twelfth-century manuscript, but references to it are found in texts from the tenth.

Gráinne, whose name means "ugliness," may be a representation of the Great Goddess in her triple aspect: virgin, matron, and crone. Although Gráinne's name seems to connote the crone aspect of the goddess, all men who look upon her see the most beautiful woman in Ireland. As a virgin, Gráinne takes charge of her destiny, choosing the aging Finn mac Cumhaill. As Diarmuid's wife, Gráinne is the epitome of fertility, producing five children.

Diarmuid is the son of Donn, a being found in the Mythological Cycle who rules over the land of the dead. Donn means "brown," and, in the case of the Táin, denotes the ox of the earth, the Brown Bull of Cooley. Diarmuid has as foster father a character from the Mythological Cycle, Oengus Mac Óc, the young god of the Brug na Bóinne.

Finn mac Cumhail's Boyhood Deeds

Some say Demne, which was Finn mac Cumhail's boyhood name, was raised in the forest by a druidess and a woman warrior. Others say that it was his own grandmother who raised him inside the giant oak at Sliab Bladma (SHLEE-av BLAD-maw). The two women raised him to be a hunter and a warrior. His skill was great. The first time he went hunting, he used his slingshot to stun a duck, and he took the live duck home. Another day, Demne and the two women warriors hunted deer upon Sliab Bladma.

"How I should like to have one of those deer," said the druidess.

"Why don't you catch one?" asked Demne.

"I cannot run that fast," said the druidess.

"Nor can I," said the woman warrior.

"I can," said Demne.

"Prove it," said the druidess.

Demne raced the wild deer. He grabbed two bucks from the fleeing herd. These he brought back to the oak at Sliab Bladma. The two women looked at each other.

BELOW: Once covered with earth, a cairn at Loughcrew today is a circle of standing stones. OPPOSITE: The boy Demne became a wise man and was named Finn when he tasted broth of the salmon of knowledge of all things.

"It is time," said the druidess.

"Yes," agreed the woman warrior.

"Time for what?" asked Demne.

"Time for you to become a warrior," said the woman warrior. "We promised your mother that we would make a hunter of you."

"Who is my mother?" Demne asked.

"Your mother was the wife of Cumhail mac Art, a great warrior who died at the hands of the one-eyed warrior called Goll," said the druidess.

"Your mother was with child at the time of Cumhail's death. When you were born, she sent you away in secret, fearing that the men who had killed Cumhail would also kill you," said the woman warrior. "Goll and his brothers know that the son of Cumhail mac Art will exact revenge."

"You are now a hunter with great skill," said the druidess. "The art of warfare you must learn from another."

The next day, Demne came upon a group of boys playing on a hurley green in front of a chieftain's stronghold. Demne joined the games. A fourth of the boys played against him, yet Demne won the match. The following day, half of the boys played against him, yet again Demne won the match. On the third day, the entire troop of boys played the field against him. Demne defeated them all, then returned to his home on Sliab Bladma. To

be defeated by one lone boy was a great shame upon the boys of the stronghold. They complained to their chieftain.

"Kill him, if you can," said the chieftain.

The boys plotted how they could achieve Demne's death.

"I know," said one boy. "We will ask him to join us swimming in the lake."

"That is a good idea," replied another. "He may be able to overcome us on land, but we can overcome him in the water."

The next day the boys lay in wait for Demne, hoping to drown him. They pretended to be swimming, and when Demne arrived, they called to him to join them. Demne jumped into the water, and the boys tried to drown him, but he was as formidable in the water as he was on land. He drowned nine of them, climbed out of the water, and returned to Sliab Bladma.

Soon after this display of exceptional boyhood strength, Demne took service with the king, but his father's enemies pursued him. Demne decided to become a poet, because poets were respected in Ireland and had great power. His father's enemies would be forbidden to harm him should he become a poet.

Demne studied with Finneces, who lived near the Boyne River. It was from Finneces that Demne took his

warrior name. This is how that happened. In the Boyne River swam a magical salmon, which ate the nuts of a hazel tree. Finneces spent seven years watching the salmon pool, hoping to catch the magical salmon. A druid had prophesied that whoever ate the magical salmon would have knowledge of all things. Finally, Finneces caught the salmon and ordered Demne to prepare the fish for eating.

"You are forbidden to taste the salmon," said Finneces. "That is my right alone."

"As you wish," said Demne.

The boy cooked the fish, but as the broth boiled and bubbled, it splashed Demne's thumb. The boy quickly thrust his thumb in his mouth to cool the burn. He finished cooking the salmon, and took it to Finneces.

"Did you taste the salmon?" asked Finneces.

"No," said the boy. "But I did burn my thumb on the broth, and I stuck my thumb in my mouth to ease the burn."

"You are the one intended to eat the salmon," said Finneces. "Your name shall be Finn."

Thus it was that Finn received the three gifts that make a poet great. Whenever he stuck his thumb in his mouth, Finn had the gift of magic, great insight, and the power of words.

BELOW: Castles were often located on spits of land surrounded by water, like Doe Castle, Co. Donegal. OPPOSITE: Irish monks took illumination to a sublime level. The Book of Kells is a superb example.

The Pursuit of Diarmuid and Gráinne

After his wife died, Finn mac Cumhail, unable to sleep, would arise at dawn and go and sit on the green in front of the fortress at Almu. He would look out over the bog surrounding Almu, the bog that kept the fiana safe from attack, and think about his loneliness. He was king of Leinster, but he had no one with whom to share his heart. His son, Oisín, and Oisín's friend, Diorruing, would follow him onto the green. It grieved Oisín to see his father so lonely and unhappy.

"Why are you out here so early every morning, Father?" asked Oisín. "A man your age should lie abed, take his time rising. There is nothing pressing to force you out so early."

"There is no one in my bed to keep me there," said Finn mac Cumhail. "Since Maignes died, sweet sleep has fled. Without a wife, why should I stay abed?"

"Father, you are the king of Leinster," said Oisín. "Surely, you can find a fitting wife among your subjects. Command me and I will go in search of a wife for you."

Finn mac Cumhail remained silent.

"Indeed, King Finn, I know of the perfect woman for you," said Diorruing.

"And where is this perfect woman to be found?" asked Finn.

"She is very beautiful, my king," said Diorruing. "You know her father, Cormac mac Art. Her name is Gráinne."

"As you know, Diorruing," said Finn, "Cormac and I have been at

odds for a long time. Even if she is the most beautiful woman in the whole of Ireland, Cormac would never consent to give her to me for a wife."

"That is not so, Father," said Oisín. "A marriage between you and Gráinne would solve many problems. You would end your loneliness, and you and Cormac would have a new reason for peace."

"To bring peace to Leinster would please me," said Finn. "You two go and ask for Gráinne's hand for me. With the bad blood between Cormac and me, it would only cause further problems were I to go on this mission myself."

"We'll leave immediately, Father," said Oisín. "Don't tell anyone where we have gone. If Cormac refuses, you won't lose face."

"That is good advice," said Finn.

Oisín and Diorruing rode to Tara to meet with the high king of Ireland, Cormac mac Art. The high king received them with a great deal of ceremony.

"Why have you come to Tara, son of Finn mac Cumhail?" asked Cormac mac Art.

"My father, the king of Leinster, has sent us to you to secure peace between the two of you," said Oisín.

"How does he propose securing this peace?" asked Cormac mac Art.

"My father, Finn mac Cumhail, asks for your daughter, Gráinne," said Oisín.

"You are welcome to ask her," said Cormac mac Art. "But I must warn you, she refuses everybody."

Cormac mac Art led Oisín and Diorruing to the place where the women were and presented the two men to Gráinne.

"These two men, my daughter, come from Finn mac Cumhail. Finn, the king of Leinster, wants you to become his wife," said Cormac mac Art. "I told them they they had to ask you."

"If Finn is good enough to be your son-in-law, Finn is good enough to be my husband," said Gráinne.

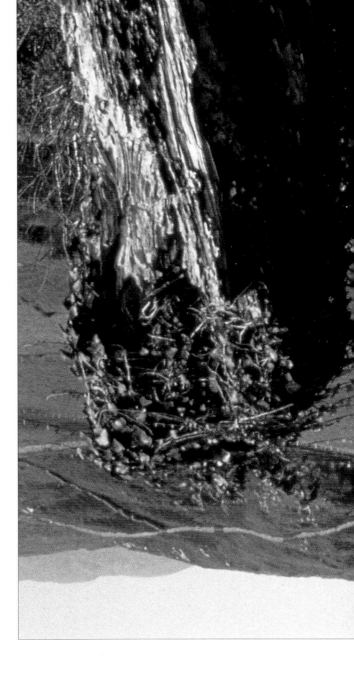

Oisín and Diorruing returned to Almu and gave Finn the news.

"Fine," said Cormac mac Art. "Oisín, return with your father in two weeks, and we will celebrate the marriage of Finn mac Cumhail with my daughter, Gráinne."

The two weeks passed quickly, with all the wedding preparations.

Upon the arrival of Finn and his retinue at Tara, Cormac mac Art held a great feast. There was music and the ale flowed freely. Gráinne, from where she sat beside her mother, watched the Leinstermen, looking closely at Finn.

"Why does Finn ask for my hand?" asked Gráinne of Daire (derry), the druid who sat next to her. "He is too old, don't you think? Wouldn't it make more sense for him to ask for me to be the wife for his son, Oisín?"

"Finn comes for you," said Daire to Gráinne.

"But he is older than my father," said Gráinne. "Who is the man beside Oisín?"

"That is Oscar, Oisín's son," said Daire.

"It would be more seemly for Finn to come to ask for me to be a wife to Oscar," said Gráinne.

"Finn comes for you," said Daire.

"Who is the man sitting next to Oscar?" asked Gráinne. "The one with the dark, curly hair?"

"Ah," said Daire. "I wondered when you would notice him. That is Diarmuid. Women love him."

Gráinne grew silent. The music grew louder. Ale cups were not allowed to grow empty, and voices rose in laughter and boasting.

Gráinne motioned her maid to come to her.

"Bring the jeweled drinking cup to me," said Gráinne. "I will make a special draft for my betrothed."

The maid brought the large drinking cup. When full, the cup held the equivalent of nine normal cups. Gráinne filled the cup with liquor and added something from a pouch she carried.

"Take this to King Finn," Gráinne told the maid. "Tell him it comes from me with my blessings."

The maid did as she was told. Finn smiled and accepted the cup. He drained it in one gulp and sent the maid back. Even before the maid returned to Gráinne, Finn yawned widely and fell asleep. Gráinne refilled the goblet and had her maid take it to all the men. Men no sooner drank from it than they fell into a deep sleep. Only Oisín, Oscar, Diorruing, Diarmuid, and a warrior of their party, Cailte, did not drink from the cup. Gráinne rose then and went to Oisín.

"It is a wonder to me that a man as old as Finn would take me for his wife," said Gráinne. "It isn't right that a man his age would marry one as young as me. I would be a better wife for you, Oisín."

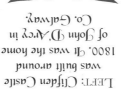

LEFT: Clifden Castle was built around 1800. It was the home of John D'Arcy in Co. Galway.

"Don't let Finn hear you say that," Oisín said.

"Will you woo me, Oisín?" asked Gráinne.

"I will not," said Oisín.

Gráinne asked for Oscar. He, too, refused.

Gráinne looked then upon Diarmuid. "What about you, Diarmuid, lover of women?" asked Gráinne. "Will you woo me?"

"You are engaged to Finn mac Cumhail, the king of Leinster," said Diarmuid. "I dare not."

"I will put a curse upon you, Diarmuid," said Gráinne. "Unless you flee with me tonight, before Finn and my father awake from the potion I gave them, I will curse you with danger and destruction."

"This is an evil act," said Diarmuid. "This house is filled with men my equal. Why pick me?"

"Because you have no equal in the hurley match," said Gráinne.

"We cannot leave Tara tonight," said Diarmuid. "The gates are locked."

"We can lower ourselves down in a wicker basket from the window in my room," said Gráinne.

"I am forbidden by taboo to ride in a wicker basket," said Diarmuid.

"Then you can vault over the walls using your spears," said Gráinne. "I will use the wicker basket." She then turned and walked away.

"What shall I do, Oisín?" asked Diarmuid. "How do I face the curse she puts on me?"

"You cannot ignore the curse she puts on you," said Oisín. "I say, follow her. Just don't let Finn catch you."

"Oscar, what do you say?" asked Diarmuid.

"You cannot ignore the curse she puts on you," said Oscar. "Go with her."

Diarmuid asked Diorruing and Cailte for their advice as well. Both warriors told him he was forced by taboo to accompany the woman. Diarmuid stood and bid his friends farewell. He went to the top of the wall and, using his two spears, vaulted over the wall as gracefully as a bird. Gráinne met him on the green outside the walls of Tara.

"This is an evil thing you do, Gráinne," said Diarmuid.

"There is no going back, Diarmuid," said Gráinne.

"There will be no place in all of Ireland to which I can take you to keep you safe from Finn," said Diarmuid.

"We shall live together until death parts us. I have chosen you, Diarmuid," said Gráinne.

Diarmuid fled westward with Gráinne. He took her to the oak stand near Connacht, where he cut the grove down around them. He made seven doors into the grove, and a bed with soft rushes in the very center. They slept, but Diarmuid did not take Gráinne as his mate out of respect for Finn.

RIGHT: Crannogs were built on platforms raised on stilts above the water. They were used from the Bronze Age until medieval times.

The next morning when Diarmuid and Gráinne were found absent in Tara, Finn was filled with great anger and rage. He called his trackers together and commanded them to find Diarmuid and Gráinne. The hounds followed the scent until finally Finn knew where Diarmuid had taken Gráinne.

"We must do something," said Oisín to the friends of Diarmuid. "We must warn Diarmuid that Finn knows where he is."

"How shall we warn him, Father?" asked Oscar.

"Send Bran, Finn's hound, to Diarmuid. That hound loves Diarmuid as much as he does Finn," said Oisín.

Bran found Diarmuid and Gráinne asleep in the wooded bower. He ran to them, waking the pursued couple.

"Finn comes," said Diarmuid.

"Let's flee," replied Gráinne.

"No," said Diarmuid. "I will face Finn here."

At that time, they heard three shouts. Oisín had feared that the dog would take too long to find the couple, so he had a deep-voiced servant make three shouts to warn Diarmuid and Gráinne of Finn's approach.

"They close in," said Gráinne. "Let's run together."

"No," said Diarmuid. "I will face Finn here."

No sooner had he spoken than Finn's voice came calling out to them. "Are you there, Diarmuid?" yelled Finn, for he knew of the warnings Oisín sent.

"I am here, Finn," yelled back Diarmuid bravely.

Diarmuid came out to the plain in front of the woods and brought Gráinne with him. In front of Finn he kissed Gráinne three times. This enraged Finn further.

"I will have your head for this outrage," yelled Finn.

Now Oengus Mac Óc, the young god who lived in the Brug na Bóinne, saw the trouble that his foster son, Diarmuid, was in. The Mac Óc flew on the cold north wind to Diarmuid's side.

BELOW: The Book of Durrow, like the Book of Kells, demonstrates the great abilities of the Christian illuminators. OPPOSITE: The Giant's Causeway in Ulster looks like giant stepping stones along the shore.

"What is going on?" demanded the Mac Óc. "Why does Finn pursue you in this manner?"

"Gráinne, the king's daughter, has put a curse on me to take her away. She will not marry Finn."

"Quick. Duck under my mantle," said the Mac Óc. "I will whisk you away from this danger."

"Take the woman," said Diarmuid. "I will come on my own if I can."

The Mac Óc took Gráinne under his mantle and sped away. Diarmuid walked out to meet Finn. As Finn approached, Diarmuid used his spears to vault over the advancing warriors and so sped away to the west. Diarmuid found Gráinne and the Mac Óc. After much tribulation, with Finn hot in pursuit, Diarmuid and Gráinne escaped to the forest.

The forest belonged to Searban Lochlannach, a giant who had only one eye. Diarmuid asked Searban for protection and permission to hunt. Both were given, but only so long as Diarmuid agreed not to pick the quicken berries which gave youth and cured diseases. Diarmuid made Gráinne a wooden house in the heart of the forest, close to fresh water. He hunted deer for her and they lived well, until the day that Finn sent men seeking Diarmuid's head or, if they couldn't get it, a fistful of quicken berries from Searban's tree. Diarmuid bested the men, but Gráinne now knew of the berries.

"What berries are these, Diarmuid?" she asked.

"They are berries from the Tuatha Dé Danaan," Diarmuid said. "If you eat just three berries, you will be filled with vigor and health. If a man of one hundred were to eat these berries, he would become a man of thirty."

"I desire some of these berries, Diarmuid," said Gráinne. "But as I am heavy with child, I cannot go myself. Bring them to me."

"I will not break covenant with Searban," said Diarmuid.

But Gráinne was insistent.

"I will have the berries, Diarmuid," she demanded. "You must bring them to me."

Diarmuid climbed the quicken tree, for Searban slept in the tree. He found the giant asleep there and woke him.

"Gráinne is pregnant and desires to taste the quicken berries," he said.

"That cannot be," said Searban. "I will not give her the berries."

"I will take them then," said Diarmuid.

"You can try," said Searban.

The two fought a long battle. Searban tried to smash Diarmuid with his giant club. Diarmuid threw away his weapons and fought Searban with his bare hands. He overcame the giant at last and picked the berries, which he took to Gráinne. From that day on, Diarmuid and Gráinne lived in the giant's tree, and Gráinne produced four sons and a daughter.

It was in the giant's tree that Finn finally tracked down the pair. Finn and his men surrounded the tree.

"Diarmuid, I know you're there," yelled Finn. "Come down and face me."

The Mac Óc saw the danger his foster son was in and sped to the giant's tree.

"Let me take you away, Diarmuid," said the Mac Óc. "You have but to get beneath my mantle, and I can whisk you away to the Brug na Bóinne."

"Take Gráinne," said Diarmuid. "I will follow if I can." And once again, the Mac Óc rescued Gráinne.

Finn continued to demand that Diarmuid come out of the tree. He threatened to destroy the young man.

"You can try," said Diarmuid. "I didn't choose this fate, Finn. The woman forced me to take her."

"This is true," said Oscar, Oisín's son.

ABOVE: Diarmuid battled the one-eyed giant Searban Lochlannach for the quicken berries desired by Gráinne.
OPPOSITE: Diarmuid died because Finn would not give him the water of eternal life cupped in his hands from the local lake.

"I don't care. I will have his head for it," said Finn.

"This is wrong, Finn," said Oscar. "You must stop this jealous rage. You will not harm Diarmuid as long as there is strength in my body. I will guarantee safe passage to Diarmuid."

Diarmuid came down from the tree, and as before, he used his spears to vault over the warriors surrounding him. He sped to the Brug na Bóinne and took refuge with the Mac Óc.

"This is senseless," said the Mac Óc. "There must be peace between you and Finn."

"I agree," said Diarmuid.

"I will go to Finn and give him terms," said the Mac Óc.

After meeting with the Mac Óc, Finn agreed to peace. Cormac, Gráinne's father, gave his second daughter to Finn for a wife. And there was peace for sixteen years, but Finn harbored his jealousy in his heart. He plotted to destroy Diarmuid.

Now it was that Diarmuid was forbidden to hunt the wild boar, the reason being that his foster brother had been turned into one. Finn came to know of this, and he found where Diarmuid's foster brother, in the form of a boar, roamed. He planned a hunt and invited Diarmuid, but did not tell him they hunted the boar.

The boar eluded all the hunters, but as it sped down a hill, it ran straight into Diarmuid. Diarmuid threw his spear, but it didn't leave a mark on the boar. Diarmuid threw a sling-stone, but that didn't leave a mark either. The boar charged, and Diarmuid grabbed its bristles and rode on its back down the hill. The boar tried to shake Diarmuid loose, but couldn't. At last, the boar succeeded in throwing Diarmuid to the ground. It charged then and disemboweled Diarmuid with its tusks. Even so, Diarmuid was able to throw his sword at the boar, killing it. Diarmuid lay on the ground as the hunters gathered around.

THE FENIAN CYCLE

"Finn, you can heal me," said Diarmuid. "Bring me a drink of water, for you have the ability to give life with water carried in your hands."

"I will not," said Finn. "Do you think I have forgotten what you did to me? I have waited many years for this reckoning."

"I have served you well over the years, Finn," said Diarmuid. "I deserve this gift."

"You deserve death for stealing the woman," said Finn.

"The woman forced me to take her," said Diarmuid. "You wrong me."

"Although I am your grandson," Oscar said to Finn, "I will not allow you to let Diarmuid die. Bring him the water."

"There is no water nearby," said Finn.

"That is a lie," said Diarmuid. "There is a well not nine steps from where you stand."

Finn went to the well and filled his cupped hands, but as he brought it to Diarmuid, he let the water run through his fingers.

"I cannot carry the water," said Finn.

"You will," said Oscar.

Finn went a second time to the well, and as before, he let the water run from his fingers so that by the time he reached Diarmuid he carried none.

"I swear, Finn," said Oscar, "If you don't bring Diarmuid some water in a hurry, I will kill you myself."

Finn went a third time to the well, but before he could bring the water to him, Diarmuid died. Finn hurried his men from the hill upon Diarmuid's death for he feared that Oengus Mac Óc would destroy them all.

Oisín in Tír na n-Óg

Early one bright summer morning, Finn and his men were out hunting. The mist was just rising from the earth. The hounds roused the deer from the shadows, and the men and their dogs pursued the fleeing herd into the western lands. It was like old times.

There was a touch of melancholy in the chase, however, for the band was much smaller than it had been. Many of the fiana had fallen in battle. Oisín's great son, Oscar, the man who had sought to shield Diarmuid, no longer lived. Many of the other heroes were dead as well.

As men and hounds followed the deer herd, a sudden west wind arose and a great light approached. Finn drew up his men and watched the miraculous sight. Out of the great light came a white horse, and upon the white horse rode the most beautiful woman anyone had ever seen. Her hair was the color of gold. Her eyes were the color of the sky. She wore a green silk robe embroidered with golden stars. She rode up to Finn and reined in her horse.

"Greetings, Finn," said the maid. "It is to speak to you that I have come across the ocean waves."

"Who are you, noble woman?" asked Finn. "What is your race?"

"I am Niamh (neeve). My father is king of Tír na n-Óg," replied the beautiful maid. "I have come to beseech from you a boon."

"Gladly would I give anything that it is in my power to give, dear lady," said Finn. "What is it you seek?"

"I have come to ask for your son, brave Oisín, great Finn," said Niamh. "I have heard stories of his heroics, and is great renown has captured my heart.

BELOW: The Land of Youth, Tír na n-Óg, lay to the west, past the sheer drop of the Cliffs of Moher. OPPOSITE: Niamh came across the waves from Tír na n-Óg on a white horse to take the great warrior Oisín as her mate.

I wish for Oisín to rule at my side in Tír na n-Óg."

"Surely, there are princes of great fame in Tír na n-Óg who have sought your hand," said Finn.

"There have been many who have sought me," said Niamh. "But Oisín's fame as warrior and as bard has won my heart."

"Welcome, fair maid," said Oisín. "I am he that you seek. I will gladly go with you."

"My son, stay," said Finn, putting a hand on his son's arm. "Who knows where she will take you or when next we shall meet? Stay."

"There is nothing to fear, great Finn. We shall go to Tír na n-Óg, my father's beautiful kingdom beneath the waves," said Niamh. "No rain falls in Tír na n-Óg, and the apple trees are always heavy with fruit. There is wine and mead and no sickness in Tír na n-Óg. Music wafts through the air. There is silver and gold beyond compare.

"Besides the glories of Tír na n-Óg, I offer a dowry of unimaginable wealth: swords of steel, steeds to match my own, hounds for the hunt, cloaks of silk in many colors, cattle and sheep with golden fleece, more gems than you can carry, one hundred young women to tend you, and one hundred knights of skill and valor to serve you. I will refuse you nothing."

"Father, she is the most beautiful woman I have ever seen," said Oisín. "I am filled with love for her. She offers me a kingdom and herself. How can I refuse?"

With a heavy heart, Finn watched Oisín mount the white horse and sit behind Niamh of the golden hair.

"Hold on tightly," said Niamh. "We must cross the sea."

The white horse bounded away to the west, treading lightly over the ocean waves. Behind them, Oisín heard his father's cry.

"Oisín, my fair son," cried Finn. "When are we to meet again? There is not your like in all of Erin. You take with you the strength of the fiana."

The sea opened and the white horse sped through. Oisín found himself in a wondrous place, full of cities

OPPOSITE: Niamh and Oisín discovered the sad lady being held captive in the fortress of Fomor the giant.

BELOW: Monasterboice, just a few miles north of pagan Newgrange, contains the highest of the high crosses of Ireland.

and castles, flowers and lights. On their journey to her father's kingdom, Niamh and Oisín passed a royal fort.

"Who lives there?" asked Oisín.

"A sad lady lives there," said Niamh. "Fomor the giant keeps her captive, but she swears never to marry him."

"I will free her, my lady," said Oisín.

Niamh and Oisín rode to the castle and the sad lady met them on the green in front of the gates. Her eyes were a deep blue, her hair golden. She welcomed them and led them into the castle, where Oisín noticed that the chairs were made of gold. The lady of the castle had food and drink brought to them, but she ate and drank nothing.

"Why so sad, my lady?" asked Oisín.

"Fomor has taken me from my family," the woman said as she wept. "I fear that I will never see them again."

"Fear not," said Oisín. "I will free you from this evil man. I will challenge him."

"A blessing on you," said the lady, "if you can free me from the giant."

At that moment Fomor approached. When he saw Oisín, he glared and set his jaw. He challenged Oisín to battle. For three nights and three days, the giant and Oisín battled. Oisín felt himself weakening from loss of blood.

"So, weakling, this is how the Fianna fight," said the giant. "Your fame is ill deserved."

The taunt gave strength to Oisín, and with renewed vigor he slashed at the giant with his sword. He mortally wounded Fomor, and when the giant crashed to the ground, Oisín cut off his head.

The women of the castle raised a cheer from the ramparts. From the exertion of the battle, Oisín fainted.

The lady of the castle had him brought inside. She washed his wounds and applied a balm, that healed his many cuts and gashes. They buried the giant and raised a

stone carved with ogham over the grave. The next morning, Oisín and Niamh resumed their journey.

A thunderstorm soon overtook them. Lightning flashed, wind howled, and rain slashed. The two travelers took refuge under an overhanging cliff. As suddenly as the storm began, it ended. The sun came out, clear and bright. The air was refreshed. A most beautiful country lay before them in the valley below. On a far-off hill sat a castle that glittered like a jewel.

"What a beautiful place," said Oisín. "What land, pray tell, is that, my lady?"

"That is my father's kingdom," said Niamh. "That is Tír na n-Óg, the land of eternal youth."

Niamh and Oisín rode toward the castle. The doors were thrown open at their approach, and a troop of warriors rode to meet them, arrayed in splendid armor that gleamed like gold. The warriors led them to the king of Tír na n-Óg.

"Welcome, daughter," said the king. He turned to Oisín, and said, "Welcome to Tír na n-Óg, Oisín, great son of Finn. Here you will be happy, and you will stay as young as you are now. Your strength will never leave you. You will find pleasure and joy here, but you will never find it cloying."

"Thank you, O king," said Oisín.

"Listen, my people," announced the king. "This is Oisín, son of Finn, who will marry my daughter, Niamh."

The people of the castle raised a shout. The king had a great feast prepared, there was beautiful music, and Oisin married Niamh. The two lived together for many years, but Oisin thought it only days. Niamh bore two sons and a daughter. One day, playing with his children, Oisin remembered his own dear father, and a desire to see Erin and Finn and the fiana made him sad. Oisin went to the king of Tir na n-Og and asked permission to return to Erin to visit his father. The king agreed. Niamh wept.

"I won't stop you from going," said Niamh. "But, pray, be careful and do exactly as I tell you."

"There is nothing to fear," said Oisin. "The white steed will take me safely to and from the land of Erin."

"Listen to me," said Niamh. "The white steed will take you, but you must not dismount. Should your foot touch the sod of Erin, the horse will disappear and you will become old and weak. You will never be able to return to Tir na n-Og."

"I swear, I will not dismount," said Oisin.

Oisin mounted the white horse and away they sped through the land under the waves until they came to the land of Erin. Oisin did not recognize the countryside, so changed was it. He looked for someone to ask where he might find Finn and the fiana. Soon, a group of horsemen approached.

"Greetings, stranger," said their leader. "What brings you to Erin?"

"I am searching for Finn and the fiana," said Oisin. "Can you tell me where to find them?"

The horsemen looked at one another in disbelief.

"We have heard of Finn," said the leader, "but we cannot tell you where to find him. Our fathers told us of Finn, as their fathers told them. There are stories of Finn and the fiana in our books, and our storytellers sing songs of their brave deeds. But these are ancient tales. Finn has been dead these three hundred years."

"Three hundred years!" said Oisin. "You jest. I left but a little while ago to go to Tir na n-Og."

"We have heard the tale of how Oisin, great Finn's son, journeyed to Tir na n-Og. It was soon thereafter that great Finn died of a broken heart. But, I swear to you, this happened three hundred years ago."

Oisin looked around in disbelief. He took leave of the horsemen and revisited places that had been favorites of Finn and the fiana. He found Almu, Finn's fortress, roofless and derelict. He knew then that the horsemen had told him the truth. He aimlessly wandered the land of Erin. He came across a group of workmen in a field, trying to lift a large stone. They would pry it up, but the stone would fall back to the ground.

"Greetings, stranger," said one of the men. "You look like just the man we need. It is embarrassing to admit that this great lot of men cannot lift such a stone. I wager that Oscar, great Oisin's son, could have lifted this little stone with just one hand."

At the mention of his son, Oisin could not refuse the man's request. He rode to the stone and, from the saddle, leaned low, grabbed the stone, and gave a heave. The stone flew from the ground, but the strain broke the saddle girth and Oisin fell to earth. The handsome, vigorous warrior instantly became a wizened old man, blind with age. The white horse, frightened, sped away, and so Oisin remained in Erin, unable to return to Tir na n-Og. The workmen, in pity, took the aged Oisin to Saint Patrick and left him there with the Christian saint.

OPPOSITE: Many Christian monasteries were located on pagan sacred sites, just as the Celts accepted their pre- decessors' holy places.

BELOW: Sheep have been part of the Irish landscape since long before the birth of Christ.

THE FENIAN CYCLE

PART 4

THE KINGLY CYCLE

he Kingly Cycle is also called the Historical Cycle by scholars. The stories contain mythological material grafted onto historical figures. Conaire Mór; Conn of the Hundred Battles; Art, Cormac, son of Art; Ronan; Niall of the Nine Hostages; and Domnall, son of Aed, are some of the primary characters. But these stories, unlike the Mythological and Ulster cycle material, have obviously been influenced by Christianity. For example, in "The Adventures of Art, Son of Conn of the Hundred Battles," sexual intercourse is only for reproduction. This is quite a different world from the Táin and other early stories. In the earlier stories, the female characters used sex as a tool to get what they wanted. Men used sexual relations to create political unions. The Fenian Cycle, too, has obvious Christian overtones, such as the fact that Saint Patrick figures prominently as a narrative device in some versions of "The Colloquy of the Old Men" and "Oisín in Tír na nÓg".

The stories in the Kingly Cycle took at the nature of kingship and explore issues of sovereignty, succession, and dynastic foundings. Kingship is viewed as a marriage between the male king and the sovereignty goddess. The goddess is depicted as a hag who becomes youthful and beautiful upon uniting with the proper king. Ireland is herself a goddess. She has many names: Áine, Danu, the Hag of Beara, Banbha, Ériu, Fódla, and the modern Cathleen ní Houlihan.

Ronan, the subject of "How Ronan Killed His Son," was a real king of Leinster who died around the first half of the seventh century of the Common Era. The story, however, has all the tragic elements of the story of Hippolytus and Phaedra, and the sense of injustice of the biblical story of Joseph and Potiphar's wife: an older man marries a younger woman who makes eyes at the man's son or at a younger warrior who is pledged to serve the king. As the stories of "The Pursuit of Diarmuid and Gráinne" and "The Exile of the Sons of Uisliu" show, this motif was popular in Irish literary circles. The text for these stories dates from the tenth century.

The storyteller looks at the relationship between the king and the land in "The Adventures of Art, Son of Conn of the Hundred Battles." Conn is a bad king in that he enters into a disastrous marriage to a woman named Becuma, who is sent by the Tuatha Dé Danann from the land beneath the waves. Conn had a successful reign up until the arrival of Becuma. The implication is that it has been successful, and the land fertile, because of his union with Éthne, daughter of the King of Norway. After many years, Éthne dies and is buried at Tailtiu. Éthne is thus tied to the goddess of the grain, Tailtiu, who dies at Lughnasa, giving her life for her people. When Conn takes Becuma for himself—an old man trying to keep the attentions of a young woman—it is considered an unnatural act. This, along with the fact that Becuma is tainted by her infidelity, leads to scarcity and want in Ireland. The land is fertile only as long as the woman is chaste and the man virile.

"The Adventures of Cormac, Son of Art" is a morality tale. It is not as wild and ribald as the earlier stories. It is polished, using a plot and developing action in ways more familiar to modern Western readers. The style and tone of the Kingly Cycle may remind readers of medieval literature and romance, such as The Legend of King Arthur.

The Adventures of Art, Son of Conn of the Hundred Battles

Ethne, the beloved wife of Conn of the Hundred Battles, died, and great was Conn's sorrow. In the years they had been married, life in Ireland had been good and the land fertile. In fact, the crops were harvested three times a year during their union. She was buried at Tailtiu, one of the three sacred burial places in Ireland. So enormous was Conn's grief that he could no longer rule. He sat, day in and day out, on Ben Etair, a nearby mountain, in lamentation for his sorrows.

While Conn was thus engaged, the Tuatha Dé Danaan, in the land beneath the sea, came together to pass judgment. Becuma, wife of Lugaid, had been unfaithful to her husband, sleeping with one of the sea god's sons. The Tuatha Dé wanted to burn her for her misdeed, but Manannán, the sea god, said they shouldn't because it

might pollute them, if not the land. They voted instead to banish her from the land beneath the waves. The Tuatha Dé decided to send her to Ireland, for they still harbored anger toward the Sons of Mil for having driven them from the country. They put Becuma in a bull-hide boat without any oars and let Manannán take her where he would. Thus she came to Ireland, to the very spot where Conn of the Hundred Battles sat in anguish and sorrow at the top of Ben Etair.

"Greetings, lady," said Conn. "Where do you come from?"

"I am from the land beneath the waves," Becuma said.

"And what is your name?" Conn asked.

Afraid that the tale of her disgrace would have reached Ireland, Becuma lied.

"I am Delbchaem, daughter of Morgan," she said.

"And why have you come to Ireland, my lady?" asked Conn.

"I have come to find Art, son of Conn. Tales of his prowess have come to me, and my heart is his," she said.

"Art is my son. I am that Conn of the Hundred Battles whereof you spoke," said Conn. "It is a pity you have come for Art, for I myself am without a wife. I was sitting here mourning her death when you arrived."

"What shall I do?" asked Becuma. "Should I sleep with Art or with you?"

BELOW: The Aran Islands, Ireland's westernmost outpost in the Atlantic Ocean, lie in Galway Bay.
OPPOSITE: Art battled sea beasts while on his quest for Delbchaem, a woman of the Sidh.

"You must make up your own mind," said Conn.

"Since you have not said you desire me," said Becuma, "let me have my choice of the men of Ireland."

"I did not say I did not desire you," said Conn. "I do not see anything unworthy in you."

"Then I will choose you," said Becuma. "But you must give me one thing."

"Anything, my lady," said Conn.

"You must send Art away from Tara for a year," said Becuma, who feared the legendary power of Conn's son.

So Art was banished from Tara, and Conn lived with Becuma for a year. The people grumbled among themselves, angry that Art had been exiled from Tara because of a woman, and then the crops failed and the cows ceased giving milk. The people of Ireland blamed these disasters on the woman.

Indeed, when Conn called his druid to find out if he knew what caused the crops to fail and the cows to cease giving milk, the druid also said it was because of the woman.

"What can we do to restore prosperity?" asked Conn.

"You must find the son of a sinless couple. We will sacrifice him so that his blood will mingle with the soil of Tara," said the druid.

"Where will I find such a boy?" asked Conn.

"You must search," said the druid.

"While I am gone, Art must rule. He must not leave Tara for as long as I am gone," said Conn.

He went to Ben Etair, found the woman's bull-hide boat, and went out to sea, using neither oars nor sail. At last he came to an island with blooming apple trees and wells filled with wine. Hazel trees stood heavy with nuts, and bees filled the air. Conn found a hostel made of bird wings and entered. There he found the lady of the house, Rigru, who with her husband, Daire, came from the land beneath the waves. They had a beautiful son named Segda.

"Welcome, traveler," said Rigru hospitably. "Let me show you to your room."

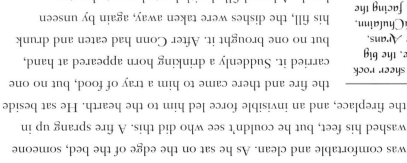

BELOW: The sheer rock of Inishmore, the big island of the Arans, stands like CúChulainn, alone in battle, facing the Atlantic Ocean. OPPOSITE: Peerless Connemara in Co. Galway catches the brunt of the Atlantic's storms.

She led Conn to a well-planned room and left him there. The bed was comfortable and clean. As he sat on the edge of the bed, someone washed his feet, but he couldn't see who did this. A fire sprang up in the fireplace, and an invisible force led him to the hearth. He sat beside the fire and there came to him a tray of food, but no one carried it. Suddenly a drinking horn appeared at hand, but no one brought it. After Conn had eaten and drunk his fill, the dishes were taken away, again by unseen hands. A barrel filled with heated, scented water appeared. There was a knock at the door, and the host Daire entered.

"Please, take your time in the bath," said Daire. "Fresh clothing will be provided for you."

The bath took away all of Conn's aches and pains. When he stepped out, a cloak of soft material appeared. He wrapped himself in its luxurious folds, went to bed refreshed, and slept a deep sleep. The next morning, Daire entered and asked how he had slept. The boy, Segda, stood behind his father.

"I slept well, my host," said Conn. "Please join me at breakfast. I cannot eat alone. It is a taboo with me."

"We have no taboos here," said Daire, "except that our warriors are forbidden to eat with anyone."

"I will eat with you," said Segda, who was not yet a warrior, "so that you do not break taboo."

After Conn had eaten his fill, his dishes were taken away and his host rejoined him.

"Why have you come to me?" asked Daire.

"Ireland has had no grain or milk for a year," said Conn. "Therefore I have come to ask for your son to help us break this curse."

"What can my son do for you?" asked Daire.

"The druid tells me that if the son of a sinless couple comes to Tara and is bathed in Ireland's waters, we shall be delivered from this curse," said Conn.

"It is true. My son comes from a sinless couple. My wife and I have lain together only once, to produce him. Thus it is with all the

"people in our kingdom," said Dáire, "But I will not send my son with you."

"That is a great unkindness, Father," said Segda. "I will gladly go, if it will help the people of Ireland."

"I will not allow it," said Dáire.

"We should not refuse the king of Ireland," said Segda.

Dáire thought it over.

"I will allow my son to accompany you on one condition," said Dáire.

"Anything that I can provide, I will," said Conn.

"My son must remain under the protection of your greatest warriors, namely your son, Art, and Finn mac Cumhail."

"It shall be so," said Conn.

Then Conn took Segda and they left the island of apple trees in the bull-hide boat. They sailed three nights and three days back to Ireland. Art and Finn took responsibility for the boy, and they all returned to Tara. There, Conn called a council, and the men and the druids came together to discuss what to do.

"We must sacrifice the boy so that his blood mingles with the soil of Tara," said the druid.

"This can never be," said Art, "I have guaranteed his safety."

"I, too, have guaranteed his safety," said Finn.

"If you are going to sacrifice me," said Segda, "do so."

The men of Tara held a sacrificial ceremony. But just as the druid was about to sacrifice the boy, he heard the lowing of a cow. He stayed his hand and all followed his gaze. There came an old woman, following a cow that carried two leather bags.

"How fare the men of Ireland?" asked the crone. "Bold men are they to put an innocent boy to death. Fetch me your druids."

The druids came forward.

"Tell me what is in those two leather bags that my cow carries," said the crone.

The head druid looked in the bags.

"There is nothing here, old woman," he said.

The crone opened the two leather bags. She took twelve birds from one bag and a one-legged bird from the other.

"The twelve birds are the twelve druids here," said the crone. "The one-legged bird is this small boy. We shall let them fight together. The winner will give us our omen."

The one-legged bird defeated the twelve flapping birds.

"The lesson is this. The cow will be sacrificed and her blood will be mingled with the soil of Tara," said the crone. "The boy shall return to his own people, unharmed."

The company agreed to this.

THE KINGLY CYCLE

LEFT: Farming has been an integral part of Ireland's heritage for more than a thousand years.

"Furthermore," said the crone, "the druids, for giving false prophecy, shall themselves be hanged."

It was done. The crone then took Conn aside and whispered into his ear.

"You must put this evil woman away. Becuma has been driven from the land beneath the waves because of a transgression," said the crone. "As long as she stays here, the grain and milk will be a third of what they usually are."

The crone then took the boy's hand and suddenly she was transformed. Gone were the withered features of an old woman. The woman of the hostel stood before them, her eyes shining. As Conn looked upon her, she and the boy disappeared.

Now that Conn was back, Art feared he would be returned to exile. He thought of how to get rid of the evil Becuma. He had not yet come up with a solution when one day, while he sat playing chess, Becuma approached him.

"You are Art, son of Conn, are you not?" asked Becuma.

"I am," said Art.

"It is a pity we have not met before this," said Becuma.

"That is through your own fault, my lady," said Art.

"Is that chess you play?" asked Becuma.

"It is," said Art.

"I dare you to play a game with me," said Becuma.

"What will you wager with me?" asked Art.

"What you will," said Becuma.

"If I win," said Art, "you will not eat until you have secured and brought to me the magic wand and the great king Cu Roi had in his hand when he claimed Ireland."

"Agreed," said Becuma. "If I win, you must bring to me Delbchaem, Morgan's daughter."

Art looked at her, surprised, for she was known as Delbchaem. He knew now that she was indeed a woman of the Sidh.

"Agreed?" asked Becuma.

"Agreed," said Art.

They played the game and Art won. Becuma left immediately and went to her foster sister, Aine, who lived in the Sidh. She told Aine of her quest. Aine gave Becuma 150 young warriors of the Sidh to protect her, and then sent Becuma to a nearby mountain where the wand was hidden. Becuma secured the wand, and returned to Tara, and laid it across Art's knees.

"Is this what you desired?" Becuma asked him.

"It is," said Art.

"Let us play another game," said Becuma, "for my wager goes unanswered."

Art agreed and they played. Becuma took many of Art's pieces.

"You have help this time, girl," said Art. "The people of the Sidh have come with you. It is they who win, not you."

"You have lost," said Becuma.

"Will you do the honorable thing and take my wager?"

"I will," said Art, "but where will I find Delbchaem if you are here?"

"You will not eat until a meal you have brought Delbchaem, Morgan's daughter, to Tara. I will give you only one hint," said Becuma. "She is on an island in the middle of the sea."

Art found the bull-hide boat that his father had taken to go in search of the boy and went to sea. The sea took him where it would until, finally, he came to an island abloom with apple trees. The buzzing of bees filled the air, and bright flowers flourished everywhere. In the center of the island was a house thatched with purple and white bird feathers. Art entered and found himself in the company of beautiful women.

"Greetings, stranger," said their leader. "I am Creide. Welcome. Where are you from?"

"I am Art, son of Conn of the Hundred Battles," said Art.

Creide pulled a rainbow-colored mantle from a basket beside her. She gave it to Art and it fit him perfectly.

"Yes," she said. "You are Art, son of Conn. I have been expecting you. Please, eat," Creide ordered her maid to bring a hearty meal out for their newly arrived guest.

ABOVE: *The rugged northern cliffs of Cape Clear Island in Co. Cork create a landscape of startling contrasts.* OPPOSITE: *Quinn Abbey, Co. Clare, serves as a reminder of Ireland's deeply Christian heritage.*

Although Creide's serving woman put food in front of Art, he did not eat. "I have come for Delbchaem," said Art. "Can you tell me where to find her?"

"I can, indeed," said Creide. "But eat first. For you will need your strength. Delbchaem lives across a great, dark ocean, in a deep, black forest filled with thorns. She lives in a dark, wooden house in the middle of that forest, guarded by seven hags who pour molten lead on anyone who comes seeking her. If the warrior makes it past the burning lead, he must face Ailill,

BELOW: Early morning sun shines over the Dingle peninsula and bay, Co. Kerry.

a giant that no weapon can harm. And if the warrior makes it past Ailill, he first must choose between two cups before he meets Delbchaem. One cup contains poison, the other the finest wine in all the world."

"I cannot eat," said Art. "which cup should I choose?"

"Always drink from the cup on the right," said Creide. "If the warrior passes this test, he must then fight the great woman warrior, the dog-headed Coinchenn (COIN-hen). She is the mother of Delbchaem. If you

lose the contest, your head will be mounted on a pike outside the fortress that protects the girl, just like all the others who have gone before you."

Art spent a few weeks with Creide, and she prepared him for his journey. After she had taught him everything she knew, Art went to sea in the bull-hide boat and sailed toward the forested land of Delbchaem. As he neared land, he put on his armor. Huge sea beasts churned the water around him, and he killed them. He made his way into the dark forest and found the hags as Creide had warned. All night long, the

hags hacked and chopped at Art, but he was not overcome. In the morning, Art continued on his way. Near the ford in a wide river, Art met the giant Ailill. They fought, but Art vanquished him and cut off his head.

Art continued on his journey until he came to a fortress of bronze, surrounded by pikes. On each pike, save one, was the head of a man. The door to the fortress was thrown open, and Art entered. In the middle of the fortress was a tall tower of crystal. A beautiful woman with golden hair came toward him.

"Greetings, stranger," said the woman. "Who are you? Where are you from?"

"I am Art, son of Conn of the Hundred Battles. I come from Tara in Ireland."

"That is true," said the woman. "We have been expecting you. Come, before my mother, Coinchenn, sees you."

The woman led Art into the tower of crystal. Her maidservants washed his feet and laid food before him. But Coinchenn, the woman warrior, knew that Art had come. She put on her armor and ordered two maids to bring the two cups, one filled with poison, one filled with wine. She marched to the crystal tower and entered.

"Welcome, Art, son of Conn of the Hundred Battles," said Coinchenn. She placed before him two cups, just as Creide had foretold. "I bring to you the sweetest wine in all the world. Choose."

The two maids offered the cups to Art. He took the cup on the right and drank the wine.

"It is most sweet," said Art.

"You have chosen well," said Coinchenn. "But before you would have my daughter, you must face me."

She drew her sword. Art donned his armor and faced her in combat. They fought hard and long. The sun was setting when, finally, Art succeeded in killing Coinchenn and beheading her. He mounted Coinchenn's head on the empty pike in front of the fortress. That night Art slept with Delbchaem in her crystal tower. When they arose the next day, Delbchaem's father, Morgan, arrived. He sought to avenge his wife's death and to keep Art from ruling the land. He challenged Art to battle and they fought all day, until again the sun was setting. Only then did Art succeed in killing Morgan and beheading him.

Thus it was that Art came to rule Morgan's Land of Wonder. Art took Delbchaem and went to sea in the bull-hide boat. In three nights and three days, they were in Ireland. Becuma was greatly surprised to see Art return, for she did not believe he would survive the terrors of the quest. Art immediately ordered Becuma to leave Tara, and he ruled the land from that day forward with his wife, Delbchaem, beside him.

The Adventures of Cormac, Son of Art

Art had a son named Cormac who became king of Tara in his turn. Cormac married and had a son and a daughter, and life was good. On Beltane, the first day of May, Cormac stood on the green in front of Tara. A handsome man dressed in fine clothing approached, wearing so much gold and silver that he sparkled in the sunlight. The man carried a silver branch with three apples of gold upon it.

"Greetings, warrior," said Cormac. "Who are you and where do you come from?"

"I come from a wondrous land," said the man, "where there is only truth and where dwells no sickness or pain."

"What is it that you carry?" asked Cormac.

"This is a most noble branch," said the man. "If a man is wounded in battle, or a woman is suffering the pangs of labor, you have only to shake it, and all pain will be banished and all wounds will be healed."

"Would you be willing to bargain for the branch?" asked Cormac.

"What will you give me for it?" asked the man.

"Anything that you ask, if I can," said Cormac.

"Very well," said the man. "I will ask three things of you. I will take the first today. I will come back in a fortnight for the second, and a fortnight after that I will come for the third."

"Agreed," said Cormac. "What do you desire today?"

"I will take your daughter, Ailbe," said the man.

This caused Cormac pain, but he agreed. The women of the court began keening as Ailbe was led away. There was much sadness in Tara. But when Cormac shook the branch, all the people were lulled to sleep, their pain and suffering taken away.

A fortnight later, the man returned.

"I have come for my second boon," he said.

"It is yours," said Cormac.

"Today I will take your son, Cairbre," said the man.

Cormac wept at the thought, but he gave the man his son. There was much weeping and crying at the loss of Cairbre, so Cormac again shook the apple branch. The people and Cormac felt their troubles eased, and they slept easily. A fortnight later, the man returned.

BELOW: *Sheep and goats thrive in the rugged hills of western Ireland.*
OPPOSITE: *Leprechauns, remnants of the ancient Celtic gods, are said to hide treasure at the rainbow's end.*

"I have come for my final boon," said the man.

"It is yours," said Cormac.

"Today I will take your wife, Ethne," said the man.

Cormac's heart was broken, but he gave the man his wife. Cormac was filled with great sadness, but this time he did not shake the apple branch. This was too great a burden to bear, he thought. He decided to follow the man.

Cormac trailed the man to the sea's edge, where a great mist arose. Suddenly the mist cleared and a great fortress appeared, its walls made of bronze. Cormac entered the fortress and found there a house under construction. Workers were thatching the roof with white bird feathers. Each time they climbed down to get more feathers, the ones they had just put in place disappeared.

Cormac went on. He found a man hauling a giant oak tree. He followed this man as he threw the oak onto an already kindled fire and then went back into the woods. Cormac waited by the fire. The man returned just as the first tree was nearly burnt up and placed yet another oak tree upon the fire. As soon as he put the oak upon the fire, the man returned to the forest.

Cormac traveled on. He came upon a house thatched with purple and white feathers. Inside the house were five fountains, which made beautiful music. The fountains flowed into a deep pool, beside which grew hazel trees. The nuts from the hazels dropped into the pool where five salmon ate them.

Cormac continued on. He came at last to a great palace. Inside, he found a warrior seated next to a beautiful golden-haired woman.

"Welcome, Cormac, son of Art," said the warrior. "Sit and rest."

Cormac sat and invisible hands washed his feet. A second man entered the palace, carrying a pig, an ax, and a slab of oak. This man killed the pig and chopped the slab of oak. He divided the pig into four quarters and placed a slab of wood under each quarter.

"Now the pig must be cooked," said the man who had brought the pig. "The only way anything is cooked here is to tell a truth. There are four quarters, so we must tell four truths to cook all four."

"I will start," said the warrior. "This pig which we are about to eat is one of seven pigs in my sty. If we put its bones back into the sty, tomorrow morning the pig will be whole, and I will once again have seven pigs."

One quarter of the pig cooked through.

"I will go next," said the woman sitting next to him. "I have seven cows and seven sheep. These cows provide enough milk to feed all in this land, and the sheep enough wool to clothe everyone in this land."

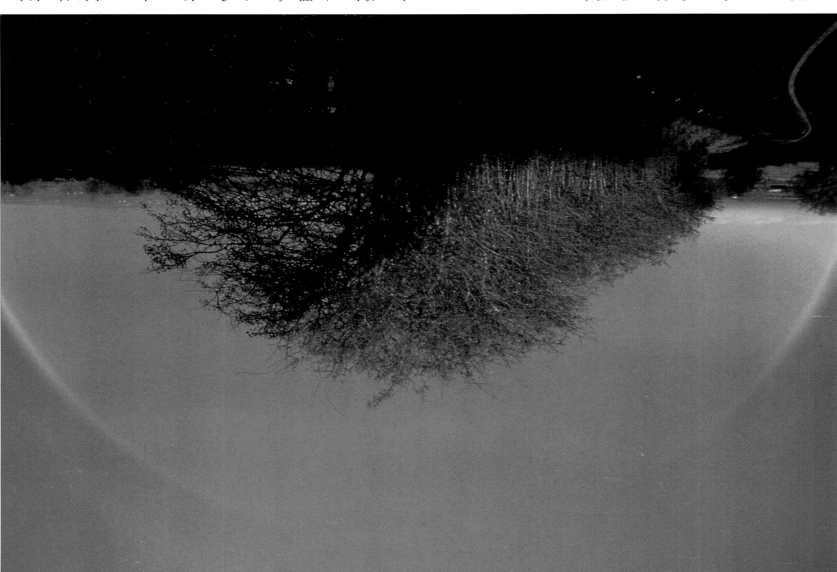

Another quarter of the pig cooked through.

"I will go next," said the man who had killed the pig. "We plowed the field only one time and sowed it with wheat. When it was ready to harvest, we found that it was done for us. We have been eating off that one harvest from that day to this."

A third quarter of the pig cooked through.

"It is now your turn," said the warrior.

"I followed a man to this place," said Cormac. "The man I followed had come to Tara with a magic branch that banishes all wants, cares, and sorrows. It can heal and take away pain. In return for the branch, I gave my wife, my son, and my daughter. I have come in search of them."

The last quarter of the pig cooked through. They ate then. When they had finished, the warrior handed Cormac a cup filled with wine. It was graceful with carvings upon it. The wine tasted sweet.

"This is a remarkable cup," said Cormac.

"It is indeed," said the warrior. "Even more than you know. This cup will break into three pieces should anyone tell a lie. To make it whole again, you must speak the truth."

To demonstrate, the warrior said a falsehood. As he spoke, the cup fell into three pieces.

Cormac was amazed by the sight of the broken cup. "What truth will make it whole?" he asked.

"Any truth," said the warrior. "And I shall demonstrate with a truth that is of great concern to you, for truly, I am the man who gave you the branch and took your family. They are here."

Suddenly Cormac's wife, son, and daughter were in the room. The cup was made whole.

"I brought them here so you would follow, for I wanted you to see this place and to learn the lessons of the land beneath the waves," said the warrior. "I am Manannán mac Lir."

"What are the lessons?" asked Cormac.

"You have seen three lessons," said Manannán. "The thatchers who worked for naught are the same as those who spend their lives collecting riches and fame. In the end such things count for nothing and are blown away in the wind. The young woodcutter is like all who work for others. He works hard but does not enjoy the benefits of his labor. The five streams are the five senses of the body. The hazel nuts and the salmon represent the well of knowledge. Unless a man drinks from both, he will not be wise."

That night, Cormac slept with his family in the palace of Manannán mac Lir. But the next morning, Cormac awoke in his own bed at Tara, his wife beside him. Beside the bed sat the cup and the silver branch with three golden apples upon it.

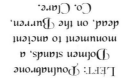

LEFT: Poulnabrone Dolmen stands, a monument to ancient dead, on the Burren, Co. Clare.

THE KINGLY CYCLE

How Ronan Killed His Son

Ronan was king of Leinster. He and his wife, Ethne, had a son, Mael, who grew into a comely young man who was a favorite among the warriors for his skills and among the young women because of his looks. One day, Ronan's wife died, and he was lonely.

"You should remarry," said Mael to his father.

"I have been thinking that very thought," said Ronan. "I hear Eochaid up north has a marriageable daughter."

"She is but a girl," said Mael. "Why choose such a flighty thing? You need a mature woman. Eochaid's daughter would be a better mate for me."

Ronan went against his son's advice and traveled to see Eochaid and ask for his daughter. Ronan slept with the girl, then brought her back to Leinster. Mael went hunting and so was not there to greet his father and his new bride when they arrived.

"Where is this magnificent son of yours, Ronan? The one I have heard so much about?" asked the girl.

"He is indeed the best son in Leinster," said Ronan.

"If he is the best," said the girl, "why is he not here to greet us?"

"I will send for him," said Ronan. "Perhaps he does not know of our arrival."

Mael returned from hunting and greeted his father's new bride, who was immediately taken with his good looks and manner. Desire for him filled her. She sent her serving maid to arrange a meeting with Mael, but the maid shrunk back at her task, afraid of angering Mael.

BELOW: *A sheep fence leans, worn by the elements, in the Ring of Kerry.* OPPOSITE: *Ronan, believing his evil wife when she claimed Mael had sought to seduce her, had his own son killed.*

"What did he say?" asked the queen.

"My lady, I could not tell him," said the maid. "I fear his anger."

"He is not the one you should fear. You will face my anger if you don't talk to him," said the queen.

The maid returned to where the young men sat playing chess. Mael played against his two foster brothers, Congal and Donn. Mael offered the maid a seat at the game, giving up his place. As he stood, she started to tell Mael her message, but the very thought made her blush, and she remained silent. Mael excused himself and left the room.

"What thought makes you blush, my lady?" asked Congal.

"I have something I must tell Mael," said the maid.

"What is your message?" asked Congal. "Tell me. I will give him your message."

"It is not my message, but my mistress'," said the maid. "My mistress wants Mael to be her lover."

Donn and Congal looked at one another in disbelief.

"You had better not let Mael hear you say that," said Donn.

"Mael will kill you if he hears that," said Congal.

"My mistress will kill me if I do not give Mael the message," said the maid.

"It would be different if it were you proposing to become Mael's lover," said Donn.

"This is true," said Congal. "Mael will not sleep with his father's wife."

The maid told her mistress all that happened.

"So, that is the way it is," said the queen. "I should have you beheaded. This is the reason you would not deliver my message of love to Mael. You desire him for yourself."

"It is not so, my lady," said the maid. "I only tell you what Mael's foster brothers have said."

The queen thought for a while.

"Perhaps," the queen said, "this is a good thing. You could endear yourself to Mael, and when you are in his good graces, you could woo him for me."

The maid spoke to Congal when next she saw him alone. Congal spoke to Mael, and so a tryst was arranged between Mael and the queen's maid. Whenever the maid came from meeting Mael, she had to tell the queen all that transpired. Weeks went by, but Mael did not arrange to meet the queen.

"You have not spoken to Mael for me, have you?" asked the queen in an icy voice. "You think you can keep this warrior for yourself?"

"No, my mistress. It is only that I fear Mael's great anger," said the maid.

"Liar," said the queen. "I tell you this, unless you speak to Mael this very night, you will die by my hand before the sun sets tomorrow."

The maid ran crying from the queen's room. She ran to Mael and told to him how the queen had threatened her. "She desires you for herself," the maid told him, "and will kill me if you refuse her."

"You lie," said Mael. "I should kill you myself for spreading such vicious lies."

"It is no lie," pleaded the frightened maid. "I came to you at my mistress' command. She wanted me to plead her case to you."

BELOW: Raising cattle remains a vital livelihood in rural Ireland, as it has been since CúChulainn's time.

"I would sooner burn in a deep pit before I would lie with my father's wife," said Mael. "I will leave this place rather than bring disgrace on my father's head."

Mael fled to Scotland, where he found protection at the king's court. He took only his two favorite hunting hounds. The men of Leinster grew angry at his departure. Rumors spread among the people that Ronan had driven his own son away. Some said they should kill Ronan and bring his son home to rule in his stead.

Word of the discord reached Mael in Scotland, and fearing for his father's life, he returned to Leinster.

But his problems remained unchanged. As soon as Mael returned to his father's court, the queen sent the maid again to Mael, and renewed her threat.

"What am I to do?" asked Mael of his foster brother, Congal. "This woman will not leave me alone."

"Leave it to me," said Congal. "I will keep her away."

"I will give you my own horse and rich clothing if you can do this," said Mael.

"Go hunting tomorrow," said Congal, "I will arrange a meeting with the queen. She will think she comes to meet you, but she will meet me instead."

As agreed, Mael went hunting the next day. The maid arranged the tryst, and the queen came, expecting to meet Mael. Instead, Congal confronted her.

"What are you doing, walking about by yourself?" asked Congal. "You will get a reputation for being a harlot. Go home."

Congal escorted her home. Still thinking that she was to meet Mael, the queen returned to the trysting place. Congal again confronted her.

"Do you want to disgrace the king of Leinster?" asked Congal. "If I see you again, wandering about by yourself, I will take your head and put it on a stake in front of Ronan."

Congal took her home again. A third time, the queen crept out to the trysting place. Congal again confronted her.

"You are an evil woman to disgrace the king, creeping about in ditches and woods," said Congal. He whipped her and took her home.

"A curse upon you, Congal," said the queen. She plotted vengeance.

Mael's father and companions returned from the hunting trip before Mael himself did, for the young man enjoyed staying behind and spending time with his hounds.

"Where is Mael?" asked Ronan. "Has he not returned?"

"I do not know where he is," said the queen. "I am sick of hearing about your great son."

"There is no harm in talking about such a son," said Ronan. "Any father would be proud of such a son."

"Such a son, indeed," said the queen. "He is not as true a warrior as you think. You are proud of the man who has been after me all day?"

"This is an evil thing you say," said Ronan.

"I have nearly had my death trying to keep my honor chaste," said the queen. "This son of yours, indeed! He has come to me daily, hoping to wear down my resistance. If he does not come himself, he sends his foster brother, Congal, to plead his case to me. Why do you think he fled to Scotland? I threatened to tell you of his indiscretion."

"I do not believe you," said Ronan. "My son is a true warrior."

"I will prove it to you," said the queen. "I will play a word game with him so that he will say the first two lines and I will complete them." Now the queen could do this because she had made her maid tell her everything that was said between them when the maid met Mael.

When Mael came in from hunting, he went to the fire and warmed himself. As he stood in front of the fire, he said, "It is cold against the whirlwind for him who herds the cows of Aife."

"That is the problem with herding the cows of the Sídh, with neither a cow to be seen nor someone to love," said the queen.

"It is true," said Ronan, as he shook with anger. He motioned his bodyguard, Aedan, to come to him. "Thrust your spear through Mael! Put the other through Congal!"

Aedan speared Mael, pinning him to the wall beside the fire. He threw a second spear through Congal's heart. The jester, mac Glass, rose from his chair and tried to flee the room. Aedan caught him with a third spear, disemboweling mac Glass.

"Why do you do this, Aedan?" asked Mael.

"You can find no other woman in Ireland to woo but my wife?" Ronan screamed at his son.

"I have not dishonored you, Ronan," said Mael. "She has lied to you. It is I who have had to flee her pursuit. This very day Congal has returned her to her quarters three times. Congal did not deserve this, my father. He served you well."

Mael died with these words, and his father was overcome with grief. The queen fled to her quarters.

The bodies of the three men were taken into a separate house, where Ronan sat grieving for his wronged son. Donn, foster brother to Mael and Congal, fled the fortress, taking twenty horsemen with him. He went to the home of the queen's parents, seeking revenge for the evil that the queen had caused. Donn and his men killed Eochaid, his wife, and the queen's brother, and beheaded all three. Donn and his men returned to Ronan's fortress in Leinster, carrying the heads of the queen's family with them. They broke into her quarters and threw the heads into her lap. At this, the queen fell on her knife and died.

Donn and his men then went into the house where Ronan mourned over the bodies. They threw Ronan to the floor, pinning him there. Donn's men riddled Aedan with spears and left him dead on the floor.

"If you are going to kill me, kill me," said Ronan.

Donn's men let Ronan stand and draw his sword. Ronan's bodyguards rushed in and a great battle ensued. The battle raged from one end of the house to the other. All of Ronan's men were slain, and at last, Ronan, bleeding at the mouth, fell to the floor and died.

RIGHT: Castles, part of Ireland's medieval past, were first built by invading Normans. The Normans, it is said, became more Irish than the Irish.